AMONG ARMENIANS

MATTHEW E. POINTON

Prologue – Tbilisi, Georgia

As I sat on the balcony gazing out into the dark Caucasian sky. I felt ill at ease. Problem was I didn't know why. I was on my travels, about to enter a country that I'd long dreamt about travelling to. I should have been over the moon. But I wasn't, instead I was as miserable as sin. So why did I feel so bad? Was it perhaps apprehension that the country we would enter the next morning would not live up to the high expectations I had set for it. Perhaps to reassure myself – or to send myself off to sleep – I read a few more chapters of 'Visions of Ararat'.

'Visions of Ararat', compiled by Christopher J. Walker, was an anthology of writings on Armenia by Britons through the centuries, a condensed account of how my countrymen have perceived that small and ancient nation that holds the great volcano that Noah is reputed to have rested his ark upon, the captivating Mt. Ararat, as its sacred national symbol.

And it's interesting how it has been perceived over the centuries since, for those who actually have heard of the place, (Armenia... do you mean America...?), struggle to grasp it. Independent only since 1991, it is also amongst the most ancient nations on earth, one of the very few familiar names on a Biblical era map. Even so, what do most people know of the Armenians? Asian or European, deeply spiritual like their ancient church or beautiful but superficial like the most famous American Armenian of them all, Kim Kardashian?

And what of me? Why was I so bothered about visiting Armenia, (after all, it's not at the top of most people's travel hit lists)? Well, I can pinpoint exactly the moment when I knew that I would be visiting Armenia one day. It was back in 2002 when I was working at the George Byron Private Language High School in Varna, Bulgaria. One of my Year 12 students was a young lady named Araksia who was an Armenian. Bulgaria has had an Armenian community for centuries – Varna has an Armenian church dedicated to St. Sarkis – and it's not the only place either. In the 21st century there are far more Armenians outside of Armenia than there are in it and those émigrés have affected world history far out of proportion to their numbers. Take the singer Cher, (real name Cherilyn Sarkisian), or the Chess Grand Master Gary Kasparov, or St. Blaise, patron saint of wool combers, or Hovannes Adamian who invented the colour TV, or Boris Babaian the computer pioneer, or Abraham Alikhanov one of the prime movers behind the Soviet nuclear programme, or George Ganjian who invented the circuit board, or Artem Mikoyan who invented the MiG jet fighter, or Ryamond Damadian the inventor of MRI and not to mention, of course, the delectable Ms. Kardashian who is famous for, well... being famous.[1]

And although not famous, I have to say that young Araksia was definitely keeping up her people's reputation. Easily the brightest student in her class, she burned with a passion for her people and homeland, (unlike most Bulgarian Armenians, she was actually born in Armenia, in the city of Leninakan), which softened the heart of even an old anti-nationalist like me. Every assignment that I received from her was a lesson in Armenian history or culture. I learnt all about the genocide of 1915, rituals of the church, of the terrible earthquake of 1988, of marriage ceremonies, the importance of Mt. Ararat and the fact that a true Armenian always wears gold and would never be seen dead wearing silver. So inspired by this latter gem was I that I even wrote a short story, 'The Silver Crucifix' about one young Armenian who went ahead and committed that unthinkable crime.

---

1 You will note here that most Armenian surnames end in '-ian'. This means "of" or "from". Thus Kardashian means "of Kardash" and so on. Kardash is a popular Armenian male name.

Year 12, George Byron School
Araksia is in the centre of the front row

And it didn't stop there. Armenia got stuck in my head for some reason and after moving to Vietnam I wrote the first of what would eventually become a series of four Indiana Jones meets John Buchan type adventure novels. 'The Lost Treasure of Onoguria' focussed on hidden treasure in Bulgaria but involved a multi-national cast including a beautiful young Armenian harem girl named Araksia and her mysterious father Zeroun whose connections with an ancient society named the Sacred Twelve unlocked the secrets to finding the treasure. And in the sequel, 'The Bukhara Affair' the heroes – including Zeroun – actually travel to Armenia where they are admitted to the inner sanctum of the Sacred Twelve where they see wonders beyond their imaginings. The third book features Zeroun again but the Armenian input is minimal though they were back with a bang in book four, 'Into the Belly of the Beast' where the grandchildren of the original protagonists secretly enter the Armenian SSR during the dark days of Stalinism.

Araksia however, was not my only, nor even my first Armenian interactions. I had several other Armenian students in Bulgaria (all bright) and once shared a compartment from Sofia to Stara Zagora with an Armenian expert on international red terrorism during the sixties and seventies, but I actually first heard of the Armenians back in 1997 when I visited Jerusalem for the first time and was surprised to learn that the Holy City is divided into four quarters: Arab, Jewish, Christian and Armenian. I'd heard the name before but knew nothing of them save that they were a people once part of the mighty Soviet Union, yet here they were controlling a major part of the most sacred city on earth. Arabs, Jews and Christians I could understand, but what on earth were the Armenians doing there? To learn more I bought and read Philip Marsden's travelogue 'The Crossing Place' whilst living in Japan in 2000. Although finishing the book and enjoying, I must admit that, at the time, it left little impression on me. I was not ready.

Ready or not, all these factors combined to ensure that a flickering flame of Armenian interest remained and in 2010 this was fanned into a fully-fledged bonfire when I travelled through Georgia and Turkey from Tbilisi to Istanbul. In a trip that included many highlights, I skirted the borders of Armenia itself, visiting many of the towns and regions that for centuries had had large Armenian populations – in some cases majorities – until the horrific massacres of 1915 ended that forever. And the places that left the strongest impressions on me were very much flavoured with a strong Armenian garnish. Set in the middle of a vast, windswept steppe that could easily have been Kazakhstan, a place at the end of the Turkish world and seemingly, when you're there, the city of Kars was a fascinating place. I'd journeyed there because it had been the setting of Orhan Pamuk's powerful novel 'Snow', a story which confronts the town's Islamic conservatism, but it is clear to any visitor that things were not always so. Many of the city's buildings betray its past as a Russian military frontier town whilst at the foot of the mighty citadel is a beautiful 10th century Armenian church, now clumsily converted into a mosque.

But if Kars seems like the end of the world, drive the 40km or so down the unmade track to Ani and there you see the real thing. Once the proud capital of the Bagatrid Dynasty, Ani is now a vast crumbling moonscape of ruins perched on the very edge of Turkey. Beyond the last of its haggard churches flows the Akhurian in a deep gorge and then beyond that a fence with watchtowers from which fly the horizontal yellow, blue and red stripes of the Armenian Republic. As I gazed out at that flag from the ruins of the civilisation that it is the successor of I promised myself one day to cross that border.

And the following morning I was due to fulfil that promise. So why feel so lousy?

At the ruins of Ani, 2010

There was also a certain justice in this trip. Unlike most of my lengthier expeditions, this time I was not travelling alone. Paul, who had had no trouble whatsoever in getting off to sleep that night, had meant to share the 2011 trip with me until he'd snapped his cartilage playing football only a few weeks before. Confined to bed, I'd gone alone, but this time he'd stayed well clear of the beautiful game and could finally see the Caucasus for himself.

We'd flown together from London City to Amsterdam Schipol and then spent an extremely enjoyable evening drinking in the cafés of the Netherlands' largest city before almost missing the Georgian Airways flight onwards to Tbilisi which we'd shared with less than twenty other passengers. Then there had been the long bus ride into the heart of the Georgian capital and a lengthy taxi journal to the dismal, Soviet era bus station on the edge of town where the buses for Armenia left from. But left is what they had already done and the next was not until nine the following morning and o there was nothing for it but to spend the night there. So perhaps that was the reason for my ill ease: two days into an already too-short holiday and we hadn't even got there yet.

Or perhaps I was just tired of work, family and home life? After all, aren't holidays meant to be for rewinding from such pressures? I closed the book and went back to bed and this time I slept.

Day 1 – Tbilisi to Yerevan

Due to the insomnia of the night before, I must confess to seeing little of the journey from Tbilisi to the border. We started off amongst scruffy post-Soviet sprawl and I awoke in a narrow river valley of incredible brownness. The rocks were brown and the sparse, hardy vegetation brown too. And at the border the people were of a noticeably darker hue than their Georgian neighbours. That I did notice and what also caught my eye was that the girls were much prettier. No offence is meant to Georgia here; I find her people to be amongst the most welcoming on earth but the girls, on the whole, do not set my pulse racing particularly fast. Judging from the border though, the same could not be said of Armenia. This was the land where Kim Kardashian's ancestors – and for that matter, young Araksia's – hailed from and it showed with a bevy of dusky, curvaceous beauties waiting in line to have their passports stamped. I smiled; something told me that I was going to like this place.

The Debed Valley through which we rattled after the border was narrow, almost a gorge. We were hemmed in on either side by brown hills, whilst below us the brown waters flowed. The valley floor however, was strewn with detritus from the Soviet era, the skeletal hulks of exhausted factories, mines and other industrial concerns, the decaying remains of a grand vision of how the world should be that never quite worked out. I was reminded of Albania, and particularly of the journey up a similar, albeit wider and slightly greener, valley from Gjirokastro to Tirana. This parallel was further enhanced when we stopped at a small roadside eatery. On my Albanian journey we'd halted at a similar establishment though here, at what was once the opposite end of the same empire as Albania, I didn't dine and instead Paul and I headed down to the riverside to gaze at the churning brown flow and drink invigorating water from a spring topped by a beautifully-carved stone. As the journey progressed it became apparent that Armenians value both springs and carved stones very much and there are thousands of the former decorated with the latter across the land, a hangover perhaps from those distant times before the advent of Christianity when the Armenian religion was based around worshipping water spirits.

The spring by the Debed

Whilst waiting at that pleasant spot, whilst not eating, I did purchase a bottle of ayran which in those parts, as in Uzbekistan, generally comes carbonated. I fell in love with ayran, the salted yoghurt drink popular from Bosnia to Iran, the moment that I first tasted in on my first trip to Bulgaria back in 1998, but Paul had never heard of it before, so I let him have a swig of mine to see what he thought. Sadly, I must report that his thoughts did not marry my own and he categorically stated that no more would ever pass his lips in the future.

The first settlement of any consequence that we passed through was the town of Alaverdi, unusual in Armenia since it has an Islamic name ("Allah gave" in Turkish). It looked an interesting place and well worth a stop, something which we considered but, alas, ran out of time for. It was a copper mining settlement and everything was built out of the same reddish-brown volcanic stone as the hills, perhaps because it is hard-wearing or perhaps because the area has very few trees.[2] There was also a rather cool-looking cablecar heading up the side of the valley to where there stands a noteworthy monastery. Oh well, perhaps next time...

Alaverdi

The Debed Valley continued both brown and narrow until just before the city of Vandazar which may be Armenia's second-biggest since the other contender for that honour, Gyumri, (formerly Leninakan, Araksia's home city), had been heavily depopulated following the 1988 earthquake. Unfortunately, our marshrutka did not head into the city itself, instead skirting it to the north, although I must say that it looked an incredibly downtrodden place indeed.

After Vandazar the landscape changed completely. Browns were replaced by greens, but not the vibrant greens of the Alps or Mediterranean, instead the more staid greens of the Scottish Highlands or wilds of Tibet. The land now was vast, windswept and empty, and snow still lay on the ground in many places whilst trees were nowhere to be seen. It could almost have been Snowdonia, almost but not quite for whilst there were many similarities, there was also something undoubtedly yet indescribably Asian about the whole scene.

We turned south off the main Vandazar to Gyumri road at Spitak which was the epicentre of the 1988 earthquake. Unsurprisingly,

---

2 This lack of trees may be natural or it may be due to the acute fuel shortages during the 1990s which caused the locals to cut down a lot of trees for firewood.

the town looked pretty new and in addition to the large memorial to those who died on the top of a low hill, we also saw rows of temporary houses built to shelter those who had lost everything I the tremor. Again, we both would have liked to have stopped and again we would have done so if we had had time to do so and so, again, maybe next trip...?

Once out of Spitak we climbed the magnificent Pambak Pass out of the valley and onto the high plateau still half-covered in snow. We rattled along the pretty appalling road passing villages which looked as if they had been transplanted from the Himalayas. Many had low houses with turf roofs, something that I recalled seeing on the steppe near to Kars in Turkey back in 2010, but then that should not have come as such of a surprise: altitude the two are similar and, as the crow flies, only a hundred miles or so separates them.

Pambak Pass

An hour or more later we dropped down from the high plateau and into the grassy, messy morass around Yerevan, an unattractive mix of Soviet dereliction, capitalist sprawl and the tasteless nouveau riche mansions of the local mafia dons and politicians. By this time though, I was desperate for the toilet and my only emotion as we rolled into Kilikia Bus Station was one of profound relief.

We dined in the bus station's canteen – cheap and with a wide range of food that you can point at – and then took advantage of its facilities to leave Paul and the bags at a table whilst I changed some money in a bureau across the road. Whilst there I spied a hotel so went across to check out the rooms and prices. Both seemed reasonable, (there were two options, standard at 7,000 dram per room per night and basement at 5,000 dram), and so I retrieved Paul and we checked both options out before agreeing to take a basement room for the next three nights. True, it was a bit of a dingy dungeon, but in a capital city it represented a very cheap sleep indeed and being next to the bus station and hordes of taxis meant that it would be ideal for getting about. In the event, it transpired that we could not have made a better choice.

Accommodation settled with minimum fuss and cash in hand, we took a bus into the city centre. Another advantage of the hotel was that it was on a major bus route and every minute or so one passed bound for the centre. We alighted at France Square by the opera house but even before we'd got off the bus we both knew that this was going to be a good city to hang out in for a few days. Driving down Mesrop Mashtots Avenue we'd seen handsome buildings with some fine architecture. Gone was the concrete sprawl and decay of the standard post-Soviet city and in its place rows of elegant buildings all constructed out of the same hard-wearing, reddish-brown volcanic stone which we'd seen so much of in Alaverdi. In Asia, here was a city that was very European and yet, not quite. The general style and layout were undoubtedly Central European yet no city on my continent uses such stone and the style of the buildings also had an undeniable Oriental element to them. And on the right there was the entrance to a very Persian-looking mosque whilst to the left a glorious-looking covered market that looked well worth checking out later.

But it was not the buildings that took our breath away, instead it was the locals. Standing and sitting on our bus, striding down the streets and now milling around France Square were, quite frankly, the most beautiful selection of females that I have ever had the good fortune to clasp my eyes upon. Now, politically correct or not as it may be to talk about such things, but I have to admit that a great weakness of mine is gazing upon beautiful women. That is, I must add strongly, as far as it goes; my religious sensibilities would cause me to suffer from great pangs of guilt were I to go any further without intending a serious relationship, but alas, Christ's exhortation to gouge out your offending right eye[3] is perhaps the teaching of His that I have always struggled with the most. And

3 Matthew 5:29; Mark 9:47

nowhere was that the case more than in Yerevan. Imagine for a moment if you please, Kim Kardashian (yes, nice thought, I know) then multiply that imagine a thousandfold and there you have the streets of the Armenian capital. Dusky-skinned, doe-eyed beauties with an absolute elegance and femininity of movement which meant that even the lesser beauties can make a man weak at the knees by the way they move, whilst their figures, elegantly clad in tight jeans or tight tops and... ok, so you get the picture. Actually you don't, trust me, unless you've been to Yerevan, you don't. But hey, if you don't trust me, then ask Osip Mandelstam, literary giant of the USSR, who described the ladies of Armenia as "women of leonine beauty"[4] or let me tell you about Paul, yes indeed, I shall talk of Paul.

Now Paul is a man whom I have known for a good seven years and whilst undoubtedly straight, his soul is perhaps not as superficial as mine, or at least, he is not as visually stimulated shall we say. The Lord's commandment regarding right eyes, I suspect, he has less trouble keeping and indeed, I even did a test on the matter once. We were walking in Wales and went into a pub for a pint and a meal and were served by a rather charming young waitress. Later that evening, as we were discussing looking at the ladies, I asked him to recall who had served us that afternoon. Beyond the fact that it had been a woman, he could remember nothing about her. I, on the other hand, am rather ashamed to admit recalling a great deal about her, even to this day. What I am trying to say is that I had never once noticed Paul engaged in the activity commonly referred to as ogling. Or at least, I hadn't until we hit Yerevan. There he did very little else and when not doing it, was forever commenting on what he had seen. I was glad, it was like a welcome to my world Paul and, of course, it helped assuage my guilt a little.

The Cascade is one of the main attractions of Yerevan. Its construction began in 1971 and it was intended to be an enormous artificial waterfall that would commemorate fifty years of Soviet rule, but when the Soviet Union collapsed in 1991 the rule that it had dished out disintegrated and thus the Cascade, like so much in the former USSR, began to crumble and decay. Renovations started in 2002 and in 2009 it was reopened as the Cafesjian

4 Quoted in 'The Crossing Place', p.156

Centre for the Arts, one of the most exciting and innovative arts spaces in the world.

It was named after – and paid for by – Gerard Cafesjian, an Armenian American who was born in the USA to parents who had survived the 1915 genocide. He made his fortune in publishing and upon retirement became a great philanthropist and promoter of the Armenian identity globally, (in addition to the Cascade, he has opened a genocide museum in his home city of New York). Armenia has a massive expatriate community which contributes millions to the local economy every year and which have helped it to become something of an economic miracle, a country which is prospering despite its two longest borders (with Turkey and Azerbaijan) being closed, its neighbour Georgian to the north still reeling from the 2008 conflict with Russia and its neighbour to the south, Iran, being an international pariah state, in addition to its own domestic lack of natural resources and good farming land.

The Tamanian Statue with the Cascade behind

Now I must admit here that, despite having a brother who is an acclaimed painter in oils, I struggle to "get" a lot of art, particular much of the more modern and abstract stuff. Nonetheless, I rather enjoyed our stroll up the Cascade as there was plenty to look at, (and I'm not just talking about the female art appreciators there). At the foot, along Tamanian Square, alongside the magnificent Soviet era statue of Hovannes Tamanian – more on him later – carved from a single block of basalt, were a series of statues including some chunky cartoonish characters by the Colombian artist Fernando Botero which I rather liked, although the ones by British sculptress Lynn Chadwick which my guidebook raved about, without wishing to sound unpatriotic, I considered crap.

The Cascade itself is like a gigantic staircase with sculptures on the various steps. You get up it by going inside the left-hand side where there is an escalator with various pieces of (largely uninspiring) modern art to look up as you rise upwards. At the top was an exhibition of sculptures using diamonds which was very Kardashian I thought, but generally speaking, it was the space itself rather than the art inside it which was memorable.

The exception to that though was situated in a subterranean gallery halfway up. This was a huge triptych of paintings by Grigor Khaniyan commissioned specially for the space and telling the story of the Armenian nation. The first celebrated the introduction of the Armenian alphabet which might seem a strange choice of subject for the central piece of a work telling the story of a nation, but it is appropriate since most historians agree that without their distinctive alphabet – as with their unique church – the Armenians would have suffered the same fate as all the other nations on a Biblical map and been subsumed and then lost in the identities of one or more of the great empires who continually lapped at Armenia's borders. Indeed, a look at the other great survivor from that era, the Jews, who also had their own faith and alphabet makes you realise that such things might well be more important that possessing land. In his book 'The Crossing Place' which explores the Armenian nation and identity around all the Near and Middle East, Philip Marsden asks Father Levon Zekiyan, Venice's Armenian priest the question of what keeps the Armenians Armenian, to which the priest replies,

> *"'The whole thing comes down to a single idea. And the key to it is the script. Mesrop Mashtots was our greatest political thinker! In the fifth century he invented the alphabet – he realized Armenia as a power was finished. If the Armenians were to survive without territory, they*

had to have a common idea, something that was theirs alone. The script embodies the idea.'

'And what was the idea?'

'Ah, you cannot describe it. If you are lucky, you will come to know it a little.' He took a sip of his wine and smiled. 'Our poet Sevak called it simply Ararat.'"[5]

The Introduction of the Armenian Alphabet

The second painting depicted the Battle of Avarayr which was fought against the Persians in 451. Although technically a defeat, the Armenians, like the Serbs with Kosovo Field, see it as the turning point in their national history. In danger of being extinguished and partitioned between the Roman and Persian empires, their stubborn resistance resulted in taxes on them being removed and freedom of religion granted, thus guaranteeing their

5 The Crossing Place, p.17

survival as a unique nation, (since their church differed from everyone else's).

The Battle of Avarayr

The final panel, Rebirth, tells the story of the resurgence of the Armenian identity from the dust and ashes of those empires that dominated it and, rather romantically, only hours after putting the final touches to the face of the final figure, Mother Armenia, Khaniyan died.

Rebirth

As anyone who has read much of my work will know only too well, I am no nationalist. Indeed, I sincerely believe that ideology to be the cause of more misery and death on this earth than any other. That said, it – like its more extreme Stalinist and fascist forms – has some wonderful iconography and I could have stared at those paintings for hours. They were busy, a mass of people, symbols and colours, and I would have loved to have been able to depict it all. Khaniyan was born in 1924 and so was educated and grew up under Stalinism with its aggressive Soviet nationalism and his art shows signs of the socialist realism of the period. But he yearned for more freedom to express a distinctive Armenian identity and because of his privileged position as a favourite artist of the regime, he was able to travel and it was whilst doing that in the most unlikely of places, that he found his inspiration.

Albania, and particularly Enver Hoxha's extreme Stalinist Albania, is rarely cited as an influence on today's contemporary artists, but it lit a fire in Khaniyan. Hoxha was a strict Stalinist, but he had also broken away from the rest of the socialist world and in order to help justify his political isolationism he promoted a policy of self-determination and with it a cult of Albanianism, (not dissimilar in both style and content to the Juche ideology of the current North Korean regime), which stressed the unity of the Albanian people despite their difference in religion, and of their continuity over the centuries, painting his dictatorship as the natural culmination of the efforts of a people descended from the Ancient Ilyrians. Thus, in the world of art, whatever was Albanian was in and Khaniyan was electrified by what he saw as "the vital connection with the genius of traditional handicrafts." The attraction to an ardent but suppressed Armenian nationalist is clear and I must admit that if there is one work in the world which reminds me of Khaniyan's magnum opus, it is the huge mosaic which graces the entrance to the National Museum in Tirana and is entitled simple 'Albania!'.

Albania!

At the top of the Cascade we stood and admired the views, (both the stunning panorama across the city and the more feminine charms in the foreground), and wondered if the unfinished section between the top of the Cascade and the Soviet monument on the crest of the hill would ever be finished, (Cafesjan's foundation is planning a museum but work has reportedly ground to a halt), and then we descended back down to ground level to enjoy a very civilised coffee amongst the chunky cartoon statues on Tamanian Street.

Hovannes Tamanian is a figure who cannot be ignored by any visitor to Yerevan. More than any other Soviet city that I have visited, Armenia's capital comes across as a single, planned whole which is perhaps a little surprising since it was established as long ago as 782BC and has been inhabited continuously ever since, making it older than Rome. However, Yerevan was never the capital of Armenia, more a small provincial town and as late as the

19th century when the Russians took over, Gyumri was the main city. Everything changed though on the 28th May, 1918 when it was declared that the capital of the First Armenian Republic would be Yerevan, (presumably because of its less exposed position with relation to the Turkish border), and between 1924 and 1926 Hovannes Tamanian was commissioned to create a masterplan for the city which would make it worthy of its new status as the capital of the Armenian SSR.

The result is spectacular and, as we walked around the city over the days that followed, we could only admire Tamanian's vision. His Yerevan was circular, part of the circle being defined by the Hrazdan River but the majority by a green belt, a long thin park, now sadly being eroded away by a number of post-Soviet buildings. But it is within the ring that Tamanian's legacy is finest, broad avenues faced with handsome buildings constructed of tuff, the beautiful reddish-brown volcanic stone; European yet also Asian in their design and ornamentation. There is no city on earth similar to Yerevan, a boast that is unique amongst Soviet cities which tended to be very identikit, and that is largely due to Tamanian's sweeping vision, although it must be added, that some priceless architectural treasures were destroyed to make room for his masterpiece.

We walked through Tamanian's Green Belt and then down Abovian Street towards Republic Square, the heart of the city, passing the statue of Kara Bala on the way. He was something of a local celebrity, the kind of guy who gives a city character. A well-off gent who grew roses in his garden, he would go to Abovian Street and hand them out to pretty girls passing by, in particular one famous actress, Arus Voskanian, whom he presented with a rose every morning as she walked to the theatre. However, he was not alone in vying for her affections, a Turkish man also loved her and so jealous did this make Kara Bala that he murdered his rival. He was subsequently imprisoned for his crime and when he was eventually released years later, his wife had left him, his house sold and all his beloved roses uprooted. Distraught, he declared that he was no longer Kara Bala but instead Dardy (literally, "sorrow") Bala. Even so, he still wandered the streets of Yerevan, now with a bottle for company, giving out flowers to pretty girls walking by. Eventually he died, found frozen one morning sitting on a rock and the whole city mourned him. Personally, I'm not sure what to make of the tale. I understand that beautiful women can drive a man mad and that Yerevan's muses are perhaps the most captivating on earth, but even so, murder is murder, and what no one seems to consider is how his devoted wife felt about it all? Nonetheless, one has to admit that the little statue of an old man handing out a rose comes as a welcome change from the usual generals and politicians.

Kara Bala

I loved Republic Square. Conceived as Lenin Square, (and originally boasting a statue of the little great man), it is the cherry on Tamanian's iced cake and one of the finest public squares on the planet. It reminded me a little of Milan's Piazza del Duomo although I'm unsure why since save for the fact that they are similar in size, the two have little in common. However, it may be a comparison that Tamanian – and to be more precise, his communist commissioners – would appreciate for whilst Republic Square, like the Piazza, is fronted on three sides by fine neo-classical buildings, the centrepiece here is not a Gothic cathedral but instead a temple of socialism, the Museum of the Bolshevik Revolution, (nowadays the State History Museum), a homage to human, not divine achievements. Taken as a whole though, whilst no single building can match the glory of Milan's Duomo,

Tamanian's ensemble, all executed in warm-hued tuff, is by far the superior space.

Republic Square

We finished off our first day in Armenia by dining at an excellent traditional restaurant housed in a cellar nearby where we gorged ourselves on fine salads, pork ribs, aubergine and several pints of beer, before returning to Republic Square to watch the illuminated fountains dance to famous pieces of classical music, a scene more Central European than Central Asian, before then retiring to a nearby coffee shop to do justice to old Kara Bala's memory by drinking more beer whilst watching the girls go by, while in the background Borussia Dortmund played Real Madrid.

Day 2 – Echmiadzin and Yerevan

There were several places that I knew I had to see whilst in Armenia and the first of them was only ten miles or so away. Perhaps the Armenian nation's greatest claim to fame is that they were the first in entire world to accept Christianity when St. Gregory the Illuminator converted King Tiridates III and his nation to the new faith in 301. As an idea of just how early that was, two years afterwards in Rome, the Emperor Diocletian was unleashing his most terrible persecution of the Christians and Emperor Constantine did not receive his vision of a cross bearing the inscription "By this sign you will conquer" until 312.[6] The second-oldest Christian nation incidentally, is neighbouring Georgia, that land being converted by St. Nino in 337.

Due to this early start, Armenia has always had a strong faith and an impact upon the Christian world far in excess of its numbers. Most notable is the naming of one of the four quarters of the Holy City for the Armenians. In 2009 during my pilgrimage to Jerusalem, I explored the Armenian Quarter somewhat and attended Mass at St. James' Cathedral, an otherworldly place, dark with incense, the rituals performed in costumes befitting some occult sect in a Gothic horror film. It was fascinating stuff and made me long to visit Armenia all the more.[7]

But the Armenian Church, whilst old, is also quite unique and isolated in Christendom. Unlike its slightly younger neighbour to the north, it is not an Orthodox church, but instead referred to as non-Chalcedonian or Monophysite. The Monophysite churches were those who maintained against the definition arrived at the Council of Chalcedon in 451 that in Christ there was but one nature, that is to say that most churches speak of Christ as having both human and divine natures, whereas the Monophysites maintain only the divine. This might seem to be an issue not really worth getting hot and bothered about, but bother about it they did

6 In Latin, "In hoc signo vinces". Many refer to this event as his conversion but in fact Constantine was not baptised until on his deathbed in 337 by which time Armenian Christianity was well-established.

7 See my travelogue 'Holy Land'.

and greatly so, the debates raging across the entire Christian world for about a century and when a decision was finally arrived at in the Council of Chalcedon, a number of churches left the fold, the first major schism in the faith, the main ones being the Coptic, Ethiopian, Syriac and Armenian churches.[8] The distinction and debate was not new to me after having visited several Coptic and Ethiopian chapels in the Church of the Holy Sepulchre in Jerusalem and an amazing 3rd century Syriac church in Diyarbakır in Turkey where the priest kindly read out a passage from the Gospels in Aramaic, the same tongue that Christ Himself had originally preached them in.[9] Nonetheless, I have always struggled to get my head around the debate; I mean, so what if He is only divine and not human? The best argument that I have heard against it is that if Christ is divine only, then how could He have suffered and died on the Cross and, if there was no suffering and no death, then what was the point of it all? That sounds pretty convincing to me though I should love to hear a Monophysite rebuttal.

But why, you may be thinking, have I launched into this lengthy, (and possibly somewhat dull), examination of the finer points of theology concerning the Armenian Church? Well, it is simple, for that next morning Paul and I hopped on a bus and headed for Echmiadzin.

The legends state that St. Gregory the Illuminator had a vision in which the heavens opened and light shone down to earth. Then, following a procession of angels, (who are always apt to appear in such visions), Christ Himself descended to earth and with a golden hammer, struck the ground three times whereupon a column rose up with a base of gold, a capital of cloud and a cross of light. Similar visions appeared on the sites where three Christian virgins had been martyred, and that then these four columns transformed themselves into cruciform churches with cupolas. After the vision faded, Gregory built four churches on the sites shown to him by Christ and the first he named Echmiadzin (literally "The Descent of the Only Begotten"), Armenia's Vatican, both the spiritual and administrative heart of its church.

---

8 In the case of the Armenians, apparently the translation provided of the Council's decision, (Armenian delegates could not attend due to strife at home), was so bad that they got the wrong idea entirely of what it was that they were rejecting.

9 See my travelogue 'Latvia, Georgia and Turkey 2010'.

Not that it looked all that inspired as we drove in. the countryside between it and the capital was being consumed by messy urban sprawl and although the 7th century Church of St. Hripsime, (one of the other sites indicated by Christ to St. Gregory), was impressive, the town of Echmiadzin itself looked like a rather dull provincial Soviet town.

Once in the Holy See complex though, we knew that we were somewhere special. We first stepped into the brand-new (2013) Church of the Holy Archangels which immediately made me reassess my preconceived ideas about the Armenian Apostolic Church. Being the oldest national church in the world, I'd expected its temples to be like those of the Orthodox: dark and dusty, ornate and icon-filled. Yet this striking modern structure of grey stone, (which I was not sure if I liked or hated), was stark and minimalistic and, dare I say it, almost Protestant in its feel. Absent were the statues of Roman Catholicism and icons of Orthodoxy and like with Protestant churches and chapels, the space was not filled with much else.

The main cathedral however, the church built upon the site that Christ had shown to St. Gregory in his vision, conformed more to my expectation, or at least, it did externally, although since the structure dates largely from the 5th century, then that is perhaps unsurprising. Inside though, and the Protestant minimalism was again evident with the main altar, rather than being ostentatious like in a Roman Catholic church or shielded by an ornate iconstasis such as in an Orthodox church, was instead simply curtained off by a large velvet curtain which, although beautifully embroidered, was still simple in comparison to the Catholic and Orthodox alternatives. By the end of the trip I had discovered that this was de rigeur although the normal decoration for the altar curtains was simply an embroidered cross. The reason for this I never discovered but in Archbishop Ormanian's 'The Church of Armenia' I learnt that "What particularly arrests the notice of the stranger who visits these churches is their aspect of austere simplicity, which is in direct contrast with the profusion of ironwork and gilding to be found in Greek Orthodox churches. In these Armenian churches pictures are unusual, except over the altars, although they are never quite absent."[10] And in this I must agree with the Archbishop for in all the churches that we visited, there

10 The Church of Armenia, p.152-3

were no icons and the few imagines of saints and Christ that were on show were, generally, of a poor quality.

The altar in the cathedral

What was not lacking in quality, beauty and ostentation were the contents of the Cathedral Museum behind the altar. There, in amongst the usual collection of bishop's hats and crooks, were some quite remarkable relics and artefacts, pride of which were two fragments of the True Cross, the spear that pierced Christ's side, (brought to Armenia by the Apostle Thaddeus who is buried in Nagorno-Karabagh), and a piece of wood from Noah's Ark which, legends state, came to rest on Mt. Ararat after the Deluge. And before one gets too sceptical about these wonders, (several spears exist, after all), the wood from the Ark has been carbon-dated to 6,000 years old whilst the spear is a genuine 1st century Roman spear. And besides, the girl who explained it all to us was so hauntingly beautiful that it is not inconceivable that she could actually have been an angel and thus it would have been mightily rude to doubt the claims that she made.

The spear that pierced Christ's side

Claims that were on rockier ground however, were those concerning the legendary beginnings of the cathedral, for underneath the main altar is a pre-Christian Pagan altar which was, unfortunately for us, shut. However, its existence does mean that, rather than being shown the spot by the Son fo God, it is far more likely that St. Gregory merely built his new church on a pre-existing holy site, thus starting a tradition that was copied throughout the entire Christian world. More evidence in favour of this more mundane explanation comes with the building itself which is cruciform in shape and topped by a cupola as per Gregory's vision. However archaeological excavations have revealed that the original 4th century church which the saint erected was rectangular in shape, not cruciform at all and possessed no cupola.[11]

11 Incidentally, the legend is the reason why virtually all Armenian churches have a cupola and most are cruciform in shape. What's good enough for Echmiadzin is evidently good enough for everywhere else.

Outside the cathedral

Outside the cathedral we had a look at the new (2010) baptismal chapel where a ceremony was taking place. It wasn't a baptism but involved a priest blessing two young men. I wondered if they might be heading off for national service or perhaps emigrating but mischievously thought that it looked more like a gay wedding than anything else. How very heretical!

The final point of interest in the Holy See complex (aside from the shop) was a collection of some of the finest khachkars from across the land. Khachkars are carved memorial stones for which Armenia is justly renowned. The name means "cross stones" and they generally depict a cross surrounded by ornate decorative carving which can be figures, crosses, foliage or geometric patterns. They are incredibly beautiful but what struck both Paul and I was their similarity to ancient Celtic crosses both in design and purpose. Many historians have hypothesised about links between Celtic Britain and Ireland and the Byzantine East in the early Christian centuries and these similarities may be a product of that.[12]

---

12 In his travelogue 'The Crossing Place' Philip Marsden comments:

Khachkar at Echmiadzin

Just outside the Holy See we spied a museum of art and sculpture which we decided to check out. Everything inside was by a single artist whose name I annoyingly failed to record. He was an ex-pat and a survivor of the 1915 genocide, something which came across in the contorted horror of many of his sculptures. Whilst much of what was on display didn't do a lot for me, some of his

---

"There are thousands of these stone crosses all over the highlands; their intricate woven patterns reminiscent of the Celtic crosses of north-western Europe. Scholars have toyed about with the idea of possible links, citing Armenian bishops who reached Ireland in the 11th century. But I suspect that the similarity stems more from a common impulse – the impulse to forge patterns from the shapeless rock – than a common historical root."

The Crossing Place, p.182-3

drawings were very good and I liked greatly his 'Christ's Descent from the Cross'.

We went into the centre of the little town which was, a few murals aside, rather nondescript and had little to keep us there. The Mother of God Church, humble beside its illustrious neighbours, was pleasant though and it serves as the parish place of worship. Dating largely from the 18th and 19th centuries though with a 1982 bell tower, it was, like Echmiadzin's original church, rectangular and simple. It had a nice atmosphere though and we were both surprised at the high percentage of young worshippers praying there.

We had an awful coffee back in the centre, easily the worst of our entire trip, and then took a bus back to Yerevan, looking out for the ruins of the enormous Zvarnots Cathedral on the way. We failed to see them but instead spied a strange building sat away from all the others topped with a plethora of satellite dishes and aerials and flying a large American flag. Was it an extension of the US Embassy, or perhaps an international school or perhaps something far more sinister? Alas, despite research on the internet, I have so far been unable to find out the answer.

Back in the capital we hailed a taxi to escort us to the Nagorno-Karabagh diplomatic mission. Nagorno-Karabagh is, like Transdniestra which I visited two years before,[13] not a normal country with normal embassies in the sense that no one recognises its independence. However, despite this international isolation, like Transdniestra – which incidentally, along with the other non-recognised entities of South Ossetia and Abkhazia, does recognise Nagorno-Karabagh – has managed to win a war against its enemies, govern itself quite well and develop national institutions better than many recognised countries since it declared its independence from Azerbaijan in 1991.

But if there is one thing that we learnt from our visit to Nagorno-Karabagh's "embassy" in Yerevan, then it is that being unrecognised by other countries may not necessarily be such a bad thing after all. My experience of foreign embassies and consulates does not encourage me to visit such places unless I really have to use their services. They are uniformly dour, serious

13 See my travelogue 'The Missing Link'.

and singularly unhelpful, as if angry that someone should actually wish to enter their precious country. And the worst of the lot, I am ashamed to say, are the british, who are so unbelievably snooty that every time I enter one I immediately feel the urge to rouse the proletariat and attempt to overthrow the established order violently. The experience that most angered me with them was when I came to use the British Embassy in Sofia once only to be told, (afterI had made a three-hour drive specifically), that they were shut for the Queen's Birthday. The Queen's Birthday! Since when have I ever been given a day off work for that?!

But the Nagorno-Karabagh mission was quite a different experience entirely. It was friendly, simple as that. Everyone smiled and went out of their way to help, and whilst things were being processed, the lady behind the desk – who was reason enough to want to visit Nagorno-Karabagh and stay there for the rest of your life – even suggested some possible itineraries, warned us of scams and pulled out a few illustrated maps. For the first time in my entire life, I came out of an embassy feeling better than when I entered and so if that is what being unrecognised does for you, then let's de-recognise a few more countries, starting with the UK.

We decided, the embassy being located in the northern suburb of Nor Arabkir,[14] to walk into the city centre. The area around the mission was nothing special, built on one of the many steep hills which surround the Armenian capital. Paul and I called into a shop to buy a drink and Paul, unable to stomach the ayran that I enjoy, opted for a strange drink of luminous green liquid. It had a picture of the plant that it was made from on the front, but neither of us recognised what it was. The only Latin word on the label was 'estragon'; later research revealed this to be the French for "tarragon".

14 All of Yerevan's new suburbs are named after lost provinces of Armenia. Nor Arabkir means "New Arabkir", Arabkir being an area in central Turkey now named Arapgir and situated in Malatya Province. Many refugees from that area settled in Nor Arabkir after the genocide.

Paul on estragon!

Weird herbal concoctions aside, there were two other points of interest in Nor Arabkir. The first was an enormous church under construction on a hillside[15] and a pair of strange skyscrapers that hung over the road. We walked on through the streets till we came to the monument that we had seen the day previously standing on the hill crest above the Cascade. This commemorates fifty years of Soviet rule and by it is a memorial to Stalin's victims, though neither was kept up like the Cascade below. What was more surprising however, was the enormous chasm between the Cascade and the monument which was a construction site. So, this was where Cafesjian's museum was to be, although judging by the state of the building site and lack of activity thereabout, it wouldn't be finished until the 22nd century at the earliest.

We moved on into the adjacent Victory Park, a classic Soviet public park now looking more than a little tatty around the edges. It had a boating lake, some statues and fine views across the city, but the highlight was the War Memorial topped by the 34m-high copper statue of Mother Armenia – not quite up to the awesome standards of the Mother Ukraine statue in Kiev[16] but still a mightily

15 Nor Arabkir Church, set to become the second-largest church in Yerevan.

16 See my travelogue 'The Missing Link'.

impressive lady as she looked down over the tanks, planes and other paraphernalia of the USSR's various conflicts.[17]

Mother Armenia

Rather footsore by this time, we hailed a taxi to take us down into the centre where we dined on Lebanese shwarma and then retired to a coffee shop near the opera house where we watched the girls go by, two teenage Iranian female tourists roller-skating in headscarves and a bin catch fire when someone threw a cigarette butt into it. Then, strolling to Republic Square, we met two local lads who, impressed by my Stoke City top (who isn't?) wanted to befriend us and meet up another time. So, we were getting to know the locals, not bad at all for only the second day. However, time and energy were lacking now and so we retreated to our dungeon hotel to map out the days ahead and catch up on some much needed sleep.

---

17 She was not part of the original design of the War Memorial. Initially a similar-sized statue of Stalin stood surveying the city from that spot until he was demolished in 1962.

Day 3 – Khor Virap and Yerevan

Say the word Armenia to most people, Armenian or otherwise, and for those who have heard of the place, there is usually one vision that is conjured up. It is of a near-perfect conical volcano, a mountain often covered by clouds but always surrounded by legends, some of which go back to the dawn of human history. That mountain is Ararat.

I know of no other nation on earth that identifies itself so strongly with a mountain. The Geogrians have Kazbek, the Nepalese Everest and the North Koreans Paektu, but it is not the same. Armenian devotion to Ararat is total and Ararat is more than just any old mountain. For starters, it is big, a whopping 5,156m high, (Mont Blanc, the highest peak in the Alps is a piffling 4,810m whilst Mt. Elbert, the highest peak in North America barely registers at 4,410m), and it is beautiful, but more than that, if you believe the Bible and legends – and the Armenians definitely do both – then it gave birth to the Armenian people. Genesis 6-9 tells the story of Noah, a righteous man, who God decided to save whilst punishing the rest of the wicked earth. He commanded Noah to build a ship, an ark, which he then proceeded to fill with two of every kind of animal. Then the Lord sent down rain for forty days and nights continually, the deluge persisted, after which the entire world was flooded and only Noah and the contents of his ark survived. Then the rains ceased and the waters began to recede and on the seventeenth day of the seventh month the ark came to rest on a mountain, on Ararat. Noah and his sons had been saved and the world could be repopulated. One of those sons was called Japeth and he had a son named Gomer who in turn begat Togarmah who himself begat Haik. And whilst the world refers to that little land in the shadow of Ararat as Armenia, its inhabitants call it Hayarstan, "The Land of Haik" for it is he that the legends say all its people are descended from.

But the story does not finish there, for descended from Noah, devoted to God they are too, but a very cruel twist of fate has been played on the Armenians for whilst they may love Ararat like no other race on earth, it is not in their country, but instead just over the border in Turkey. And as the border between those two ancient neighbours is closed due to Turkey refusing to admit that the events of 1915 were a genocide – and because of Armenia's involvement in the Nagorno-Karabagh conflict – then the sad fact is that whilst all Armenians may look at Ararat, it is almost impossible for them to visit it.

We had tried to see the sacred mountain twice. On a clear day it is visible from Yerevan, but neither of the past two days had been clear and all we'd seen were the lower slopes before a blanket of cloud took over. However, the view from Yerevan is not the one that all Armenians treasure, instead it is another which graces a thousand postcards and posters and even the cover of the book that I was reading. The view of Ararat, the image of Armenia is of the sacred peak looming in the distance and the monastery of Khor Virap standing in the foreground.

Khor Virap and Ararat on the cover of 'The Crossing Place'

Khor Virap stands some 43km south of Yerevan in the (appropriately named) Ararat Province. It was founded back in the 5th century but architecturally it is of no great interest, the present structure dating from the 17th century. Its main obvious attraction is how stunning it looks with Ararat as a backdrop, but there is more to it than that, for it is also one of Armenia's holiest sites, being built over the snake-infested pit where St. Gregory the Illuminator, (yes, he of Echmiadzin fame), was imprisoned for thirteen years in the 3rd to 4th centuries by King Tiridates II before finally being hauled out because the king had gone mad and his followers thought that it might have been imprisoning a holy man that did it. Gregory then went ahead and cured the crazy king and in doing so converted his former tormentor – and by extension, his people – to the Christian faith.

We journeyed out in the taxi that we had taken the previous evening back to our hotel as he'd offered us a decent price and using public transport would have been extremely time consuming. I was beginning to learn some of the advantages of travelling with another. Alone, the asking price would have been unthinkable, but shared between two it was quite reasonable.

The short journey to the monastery was unremarkable, across a narrow strip of flat land sandwiched in-between the cloud-shrouded slopes of Ararat to the right and the Lesser Caucasus to the left. Arriving at the monastery we had climb up a few steps before entering the small, fortified compound. The church itself was a disappointment. It was dark, damp and dull, the large curtain across the altar emblazoned with a gold cross being the only decoration. Both Paul and I felt little there but, unlike most monasteries, the church was not why we had come here. Instead we stood on the ramparts and looked out over the magnificent view of Armenia's holy mountain.

Ararat was, annoyingly, covered in cloud the whole time, although the peak did appear briefly at one point. Even so, it was still an awe-inspiring sight but, more than that, for me, it was also unexpected.

As I've said before, I've long been fascinated with Armenia and used the country as the setting for several of my novels. In two of them – 'The Bukhara Affair' and 'Into the Belly of the Beast' the heroes visit a secret underground complex run by the Sacred Twelve located in caverns inside Mount Ararat. Which is all well and good except that, stood on the ramparts of the monastery, I realised that it isn't built on the foothills of Ararat as it appears in the pictures, but is instead a good few miles from the mighty mountain with several Turkish villages, all boasting mosques with their tell-tale pencil minarets, in the way. And the border between the two countries runs right by the monastery, literally a field away, where a barbed wire fence with watchtowers scars the landscape. To my dismay I discovered that a whole section of my novel was totally infeasible and would have to be rewritten.

Our taxi driver beckoned us to a small side chapel and then pointed to a hole in the floor with a ladder attached. Momentarily I was confused, but then I realised: it led down to the pit in which St. Gregory the Illuminator had suffered for thirteen long years.

Descending in a fashion clearly contravening UK Health and Safety legislation, I entered the bell-shaped chamber where the saint had once languished. This was far more moving than the church above for although not unpleasant for a few minutes, I am sure that I would go stir crazy if I spent more than a day in such a place. Yet from this prison Gregory had evangelised an entire nation. I knelt before his image and prayed.

Praying in St. Gregory's Prison

After the pit, our driver took us out of the monastery compound and up a small hillock nearby. On the top there were a couple of bedraggled-looking thorn bushes to which the devout had tied scraps of material. This practice I have witnessed at both Christian and Pagan sites across Georgia, Turkey and Bulgaria and it is undoubtedly a Pagan practice preceding all the modern religions. Then he showed us the view: Yerevan to the north, Ararat to the west and, in-between the mountain and the monastery, the thin silver ribbon of the Arax River which forms the border between modern-day Turkey and Armenia, (and before that the Russian and Ottoman empires). I smiled for when I had first learnt about this land and its people all those years ago in a classroom in Bulgaria, I had asked Araksia what her unusual name meant and she had replied, "It is the name of a river in Armenia."

Khor Virap with the Turkish border behind

Back in Yerevan we headed first to the Nagorno-Karabagh diplomatic mission to pick up our passports now freshly-stamped with colourful Nagorno-Karabagh visas. Then we had our taxi drop us off at the nearby Genocide Memorial.

Prior to the First World War, the Armenians had not had a state of their own, instead being scattered across the Russian and

Ottoman Empires, (and to a lesser extent, Persia), as well as there being a significant diaspora beyond.

In each of the two empire, around two millions Armenians lived. Theirs was not a privileged position in either since they did not subscribe to the state religion: Sunni Islam for the Ottomans and Orthodox Christianity for the Russians, but their position in Russia was slightly better and in both they had done well economically which, as the Jews can attest only too well, can be both a blessing and a curse. The Ottoman Empire had such a strong Armenian heritage because, in addition to occupying some provinces of Eastern Armenia, it also included within its lands, the old Western Armenia, Cilicia, a word which one encounters all the time in modern-day Armenia, be it in the name of Yerevan's largest bus station to the most popular brand of beer. These Armenians had lived beside their Muslim neighbours as separate dhimmi[18] for centuries, but the nationalist movements of the late 19th and early 20th centuries had begun to sour relations and pogroms began to occur with increasing regularity. Then, as World War I began with the Ottomans on the German side fighting the British at Gallipoli and in Arabia and the Russians in the east, matters began to get serious. The empire had been in decline for years, losing 33% of its territory between 1908 and 1912 and, significantly, that had almost all been to the Christians in the Balkans and their departure from the empire meant that the Armenians remained as the only major Christian group left within its borders. In 1915 the Russians, despite being driven back on all other fronts, were inflicting defeat after defeat on the poorly led, organised and equipped Ottomans and many of those fighting in the Russian ranks were Armenian volunteers from Russian Armenia eager to liberate their homeland from the Muslims. Paranoia about "the enemy within" was whipped up and the sixty thousand Armenians in the Ottoman armed forces were transferred to labour battalions and stripped of their weapons. Within three months all had been massacred. Orders were also given to move the Armenians living near to the front into the Syrian Desert. Forced marches, massacres and the unforgiving terrain killed almost all of them and many more too, for virtually all Armenians, whether close to the front or not, were

18 The dhimmi system was one of the foundation stones upon which the Ottoman Empire had been built. The term is often translated as "nation" or "minority" and under the system recognised dhimmi had certain rights and obligations different to those of the ruling Muslims. Recognised dhimmi were religious rather than nations in the modern sense of the word. Therefore, Jews, Greeks (i.e. Orthodox Christians), and Armenians were three of the most significant dhimmi in the Ottoman Empire. I discuss the system in some length in my travelogue 'Balkania'.

deported. By the end of the war one and a half million Armenians had died.

That is fact and is undisputed. The rest though, is, even today, the cause of the bitterest debate. Turkey, the successor state to the Ottoman Empire will neither accept any responsibility nor admit that there was a genocide. They cite, correctly, that around 600,000 Turks also died, (largely slaughtered by Armenians who had captured the depopulated lands), and that the new state was not the old and so should not bear its guilt. More controversially, they insist, despite evidence to the contrary, that the deportations and murders were not organised or planned from the centre and instead local militias did the killing of their own volition. More interestingly, there are the arguments put forward in Taner Akçam's 'A Shameful Act', (which I was reading on the trip), that Atatürk had not pressed the issue of Turkish guilt because many of those responsible were the very same nationalists who had helped him to overthrown the old Ottoman order and establish his Turkish Republic. Whatever the case, even to this day, many countries including, I am deeply ashamed to say, my own, refuse to acknowledge the Armenian genocide and no reparations of either land or money or even an apology have ever been made. But what does this matter you may ask? Well, when outlining his own murderous ambitions, a certain Adolf Hitler reassured his generals that all would be alright with the words, "Who still talks nowadays of the extermination of the Armenians?" Ignoring or forgetting one genocide merely encourages another.

The memorial, built to ensure that the Armenians who survived will never ignore or forget it, is set on a hillside across the Hrazdan River from the city centre. It consists of a 100m long memorial wall with all the names of the towns and villages in Turkey where the massacres took place engraved upon it. Then there is a tall spike which symbolises the rebirth of the Armenian people – but is riven in two to symbolise the separation of Western and Eastern Armenia, (the effect of which was somewhat ruined during our visit as the spike was covered in scaffolding) – and then finally there is a ring of twelve, inward-leaning basalt slabs, reminiscent of khachkars, which represent the twelve lost provinces of Western Armenia, their bowed position suggesting figures in mourning. And in the middle of them, 1.5m below, is the eternal flame where roses are laid by those wishing to pay their respects. We both found it extremely moving and stayed there for some time as mournful traditional tunes played over loudspeakers and the wind flickered the flame.

The Genocide Memorial

Away from the memorial itself, there are two other parts to the complex. Annoyingly, the museum was closed for renovations, but we wandered among the trees planted by visiting dignitaries such as the Pope, Vladimir Putin and Georgi Purvanov, the Bulgarian President.

We dined at a nearby restaurant on excellent traditional fayre and then took a taxi into the centre, getting out on Mesrop Mashtots Avenue as there were two places that I very much wanted to check out there. The first was the gorgeous covered market, built in the 1940s and boasting an amazing frontage covered with traditional Armenian decorations. I was dismayed when we entered though, to discover that it had been transformed into an upmarket shopping centre with large plastic butterflies hanging from the roof. Progress, eh?

The Covered Market

The second site of interest proved to be far more rewarding. The city's mosque, reached through an ornate blue-tiled gateway, is a little piece of Iran in Armenia. Built in 1765, it is a tranquil oasis of calm in the midst of the city which reminded me of some of the great mosques that I visited in Uzbekistan. Also of interest was a display in its precincts, (provided by the Iranian government), or Persian artefacts, the favourite of which for me was a paper-thin porcelain plate.

Yerevan Mosque

Our last stop of the day was the State History Museum in Republic Square. Paul was not overly interested in museums, but we both thought that this one might give us a good overview that we were setting off through the following day and so it proved. We saw artefacts and exhibitions from all ages of Armenia's history, (and there were a lot of them), with my personal highlights including a preserved Bronze Age wooden cart and an incredible scale model of the ruins of Ani, several metres across. Having explored the site on foot during my journey through Eastern Turkey in 2010[19] it was great to get an overview and revisit all those incredible ruins, like Ararat another of the symbols of Armenia that can now only be gazed at from over a border fence.

By this time we had had all the culture – and walking – that we could manage so we retired to the Café of the Burning Bin where we'd sipped coffee before to indulge in a new passion. Paul is a passionate chess player and had repeatedly pestered me to play the game with him, but the problem is that most matches last far too long for anything less than a trip on the Trans Siberian, so instead I had introduced him to backgammon the previous evening, the staple of my lengthy Trans-Asian Expedition with the Lowlander in 2002.[20] To my delight, my new travelling companion found the game as much to his taste as my old one had, but, inexplicably, the owners of the coffee shop did not and so, losing our custom for all eternity, we decamped across the square to another establishment overlooking the small ornamental lake and, on the table next to a local mafia heavy and his lithe young lady, we played a couple of games and gave these more deserving proprietors our business before returning back to our dungeon hotel to turn in early in anticipation of the early start on the morrow.

19 See my travelogue 'Latvia, Georgia and Turkey 2010'.
20 See my travelogue 'Across Asia With A Lowlander'.

Day 4 – Yerevan to Sisian

We awoke early for our investigations the previous evening had revealed that the marshrutka for Sisian departed at 08:30. After several days in and around Yerevan we were heading south, going to see something of the country beyond the capital and I'd chosen Sisian as our next stop since it looked interesting and was the lion's share of the way down to Stepanakert, the capital of Nagorno-Karabagh, our final destination. It was to be an epic journey which, on a marshrutka, neither of us was looking forward to all that much. 208km in all, that doesn't sound much, a similar distance from my home town to London in fact, but Armenia is not the UK where you can jump on a high speed train and whiz down there in an hour and a half. Our anticipated arrival time was 2pm and five hours on a marshrutka is never a prospect to be welcome.

We dined on pastries and coffee in the bus station, served by the most miserable girl on the planet, (Paul and I suspected and thus thing (like us) out of her routine were difficult to cope with), and then boarded the service driven by the second-most miserable person on the planet. Also travelling with us was the local alcoholic who, despite the early hour, was already knocking back the beers. He tried to befriend us. I, anti-social git that I can be when I choose, flatly ignored him. Paul, a far nicer and politer gent, tried to hold a conversation and beer pressed into his face. The driver was none too impressed but Paul's new pal was all smiles and laughter. Half an hour after the scheduled time, we set off.

The first part of the journey was along the narrow plain which we had travelled down en route to Khor Virap. It was a nondescript landscape, the outskirts of the city littered with the ruins of dead industry. Near to the famous monastery we stopped to fill-up, a most unusual experience indeed. At the gas station, everyone was ordered off the bus and told to stand well away. Then the vehicle was refuelled, not with petrol or diesel but instead with gas, deposited into a large cylinder that was worryingly situated beneath my seat. This took considerably longer than a standard fill-up and I wondered why things were done this way, (I have witnessed it nowhere else on my travels), for all the cars and lorries seemed to be fuelled in this fashion. What is more, it smelt and the smell lingered after we had all piled on again, although after ten minutes or so the odour faded.

The scenery continued much the same down as far as Yeraskh at which point the Arax Valley continued onwards south-east but we veered off and upwards to the east. The reason was that to the south lay Nakhijevan, an enclave of Azerbaijan sandwiched in-between Iran and Armenia. I wondered how it ever survived in tact during the war between Armenia and Azerbaijan during the early nineties and perhaps the steep mountainous terrain provides the answer: any potential territorial gains would come at great human cost. Like the rest of Azerbaijan, the border with Armenia is closed and so all traffic to the enclave has to go through Iran – hardly a state at the heart of international friendliness – and so I imagine that achieving any kind of economic growth there must be very hard indeed.

Nakhijevan from the marshrutka

Between Yeraskh and Yeghegnadzor we climbed and climbed, through nut brown and barren hills up onto the high mountain plateau where snow still lay on the ground in places. We were now in the heart of the Lesser Caucasus and it was beautiful. Things were less beautiful on the marshrutka itself however since, now feeling rather worse for wear, near to Yeghegnadzor, Paul's drunk friend proceeded to vomit all over a fellow passenger. The man in question, understandably, none too happy about this, particularly as he was wearing a new shirt. The marshrutka stopped by the river, the man proceeded to clean himself up and the driver, now even crankier than before, smacked the drunk around the head which rather upset Paul. I continued to read 'A Shameful Act' until the whole pathetic charade was over.

Driving along the Arpa and Vorotan valleys high up in the mountains was a great experience. It was a bleak place with little vegetation and fewer inhabitants, almost reminiscent of the Scottish Highlands. I noticed near to Zangezour a mine to our right. Marsden visited this facility in 'The Crossing Place' and descended the shaft. It was interesting because Armenia has few mineral resources and this establishment was in fact sunk to mine water. It was all part of a grand project to divert water from the Arpa and Vorotan via two underground tunnels (hence the mine) 49km and 22km long respectively into Lake Sevan in order to try and raise its water levels following an ecologically disastrous scheme implemented under Stalin which had caused the water levels to drop by 18m. It was an impressive endeavour to right a wrong, although so far the success has only been partial.

The water mine

We reached Sisian just after two. It was a small town nestled in a valley several kilometres off the main road. Glad to be off the marshrutka at last, we first booked ourselves into Hotel Drina, the classiest, (and at around €25 per night, the most expensive), sleep of the entire trip, although, to be fair, the competition for that particular honour wasn't stiff.

Next door was a post office so we decided to send off all our postcards but, bizarrely, it didn't sell stamps (???), so instead we arranged for a taxi to take us to the region's Number One tourist attraction: Karahunj.

Karahunj is sometimes referred to as Armenia's Stonehenge. That's because it's a very old (circa 2,000BC) collection of stones, some of which are arranged in a circle. Whether it's as good as Stonehenge I cannot say, not having visited my own country's most famous prehistoric monument, but it almost certainly receives less visitors. When we arrived we were the only tourists – and indeed, our driver aside, people around for miles. We wandered about the standing stones wondering what they were put there for, (archaeologists haven't got a clue). From what I could gather, there was a ring of stones with several lines of stones going off it. Whatever the purpose of it all, Karahunj was amazing, just as much because of its setting on a windswept moor with 360° views of snow-capped peaks and hardly a human habitation in sight.

Bleak isolated majesty: Karahunj

Back in the town, we decided to check out the museum but couldn't find it and so instead walked through the streets to the

Monastery of Syumi. On the way we passed an incredible war memorial with two friezes depicting soldiers going into battle and another of a very Soviet-looking displaying the bounty of the fields. What intrigued me though, was which war it was that the monument commemorated? The date on the memorial was 1921 yet who were the Soviets fighting then? Turkey? Persia perhaps? Or was it part of the Russian Civil War? Research on the internet eventually revealed the answer. It was the campaign against the romantically-named Republic of Mountainous Armenia. After the Civil War, the USSR had looked to sovietise Russia's South Caucasian colonies. The Red Army entered Armenia on the 29th November 1920 and on the 2nd December the transfer of power from the Republic of Armenia to the USSR took place, (one presumes that the main reason behind this was that the Armenians knew that they would struggle to beat the Soviets and the prospect of a Turkish occupation only five years after the genocide was unthinkable). However, in the discussions between the Soviets and the Dashnaks (Armenian nationalists) a stumbling block was hit when the Soviets declared their intention to transfer Nagorno-Karabagh and Syunik, (the slither of Armenia between Nakhijevan and Nagorno-Karabagh), to the Azerbaijani SSR. With neither side willing to budge, on 18th February 1921, the Dashnaks led an anti-Soviet rebellion in Yerevan which succeeded in taking control of the city and surrounding areas for forty-two days before being crushed by the numerically-superior Red Army. Then the Dashnaks, under their leader Garegin Nzhdeh, retreated to Syunik and on 26th April 1921 the Republic of Mountainous Armenia was declared in Tatev Monastery with Goris as its capital.

Undeterred, the Red Army conducted massive military operations, striking at the rebels from both the north and the east and, after several months of fierce fighting, the Dashnaks capitulated in July 1921 after the Soviets agreed to keep both Syunik and Nagorno-Karabagh within the Armenian SSR, a promise that becomes crucial when looking at the conflict over the latter province seventy years later. By then that earlier war had been all but forgotten save by a few Armenian patriots and those who pass by and pause at the incredible monument in Sisian.

Friezes on the war memorial

Across the street from the monument was a drinking fountain flanked by two amazing carved dragons. The style fascinated me, neither European nor Asian, but wholly unique, wholly Armenian and more like Aztec art than anything else I've ever seen.

An almost Aztec dragon

We walked up through the backstreets to Syuni Monastery, although these days only the church remains. That though, is well worth seeking out, a beautiful building dating from the 6th century when it was built by no less a figure than Princess Varazdukht (whoever she was). Inside, like all Armenian churches, it was dark and simple, the great curtain covering the altar but also, surprisingly, the interior was circular whereas the exterior is a rectangle. This, it seems, is a common feature of Armenian church architecture:

> *"The dank chambers of churches have always vied with the Armenians' earthier more oriental beliefs. But in one respect these extraordinary buildings are defiantly Armenian. Nowhere else do churches - nor, to my knowledge, buildings of any kind – look as different outside as they do inside. What outside is angular and pointed, inside is round; where outside there is a sharp cone, inside is a cupola; outside triangular blind niches, inside tubular alcoves and apses; outside a pitch roof, inside barrel-vaults or arcing rib-vaults. Looking at the ground plan of these churches, they appear almost like two buildings in one. By using walls in-filled with rubble the Armenian masons seem to have been presenting some sort of deliberate enigma."*[21]

Syuni Monastery

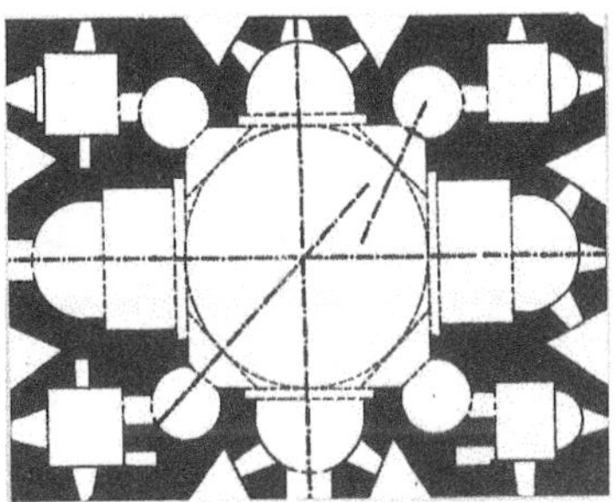

Plan of Syuni Monastery

What made Syuni Monastery all the more memorable though was the extremely friendly churchwarden who showed us the church's finest treasures: a set of sculptures by Edward Ter-Ghazarian. Ghazarian is internationally famous as the master of the micro sculpture and his works are so small that he has to use a microscope to create them. Under a magnifying glass in the church we viewed sculptures made on a strand of human hair, half a rice

---

21 The Crossing Place, p.191

seed, a small piece of ivory and thin tin plate. I can honestly say that I have never seen anything else quite like them.

Outside the church rows of ordered, new graves marked the final resting places of scores of young soldiers from the Nagorno-Karabagh conflict, the place where we would be travelling to the next day. It reminded me of a similar cemetery that I once walked around in Višegrad in Bosnia, and like that place it was sad. Young lives cut short unnecessarily is never glorious.

The grave of a 19-year old soldier

That evening we dined Soviet-style in the former Inturist hotel, the only customers in the vast restaurant that had seats for two hundred. Still, the food was excellent. Then we took our backgammon board and hit the town, heading over the bridge that traverses the Vorotan to the town's only bar and there we drank and played the night away in deepest, darkest Armenia.

Day 5 – Sisian to Stepanakert and Vandazar

We awoke that morning knowing that, by the afternoon, we would be in a different country. That was a definite. What was less clear however, was which country that would be.

The visas in our passports declared 'Artsakh' which is the Armenian name for Nagorno-Karabagh. However, according to any world map, (or at least any map produced outside of Armenia), there is no such country as Artsakh or Nagorno-Karabagh and instead the city that we were headed for, Stepanakert – marked as Khankendi on most maps – is place firmly inside Azerbaijan. So, is it Nagorno-Karabagh or Azerbaijan, what's the difference and why was there so much fighting about it in the early 1990s?

The Armenians have lived in the region for millennia, but so have many other races such as the Azeris, Georgians, Kurds and several more. That's all well and good except that often one race did not dominate the entire region. Instead you might get one Armenian village, then a Kurdish one, then an Azeri one and so on. To see what I mean, take a look at this ethnic map of Nagorno-Karabagh prior to the conflict.

ETHNIC COMPOSITION OF THE NAGORNO-KARABAKH AUTONOMOUS OBLAST IN 1989

That said, by the start of the 20th century, the area that nowadays comprises Armenia was predominantly Armenian, that of Nakhijevan was largely Azeri and that of Nagorno-Karabagh, largely Armenian, which explains why the Dashnaks fought so hard against the Red Army to have both Syunik and Nagorno-Karabagh included within the new Armenian SSR, (but not Nakhijevan); after all, they'd just lost half their traditional homelands to the Turks who had ethnically cleansed the lot.

Under Stalin though, things were different and it didn't matter much which SSR you were in as everything was dictated by the centre. So it was that, almost immediately after defeating the Republic of Mountainous Armenia, Nagorno-Karabagh (but not Syunik) was given to the Azerbaijani SSR and then, two years later, given a special autonomous status within Azerbaijan, hence the Nagorno-Karabagh Autonomous Region was born, (a little like Kosova in Yugoslavia and we all know how that one ended up as well). The question begs as to why did Stalin renege on his deal with the Dashnaks and do this? The answer is a simple one, namely that it was entirely logical both in terms of internal economics and international relations. Internally, it meant that farmers could continue doing what they had always done and move their flocks between the plains of Azerbaijan and highlands of Nagorno-Karabagh according to the seasons, (Nagorno-Karabagh lies on the Azerbaijani side of the watershed). Internationally, the USSR were courting Kemalist Turkey at the time as a prospective ally, believing that Atatürk would turn his new republic into a communist state and the Turks naturally supported their Muslim Turkic brothers the Azeris over the old enemy, the Armenians who had no international friends.[22]

However, when drawing up the border for the new Nagorno-Karabagh Autonomous Region two years later, instead of keeping the pre-existing boundaries of the province, the Soviets redrew them to give the region an overwhelmingly Armenian population, with the city of Shusha being the only major Azeri enclave, (largely because its Armenian population had all been murdered by the Azeris in 1920). And the new autonomous region they kept permanently separated from the Armenian SSR by creating another autonomous region, Red Kurdistan, in-between the two. This was a short-lived attempt to inspire Kurdish loyalty to the USSR which failed largely due to there being virtually no Kurds – and precious few other people it must be said – in the inhospitable strip of mountainous terrain that the new autonomous region consisted of. Thus, in 1929 Red Kurdistan was abolished and Nagorno-Karabagh became an Armenian island marooned within the Azerbaijani SSR.

22 The Caucasus, p.105

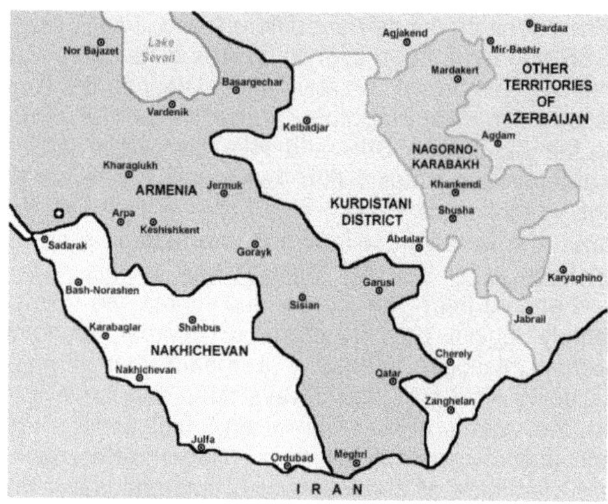

- Kurdistani District (Red Kurdistan), part of Azerbaijanian SSR in 1930
- Nagorno-Karabakh Autonomous Province, part of Azerbaijanian SSR
- Nakhichevan Autonomous Republic, part of Azerbaijanian SSR
- other territories of Azerbaijanian SSR
- Armenian SSR

And thus things continued until perestroika and the gradual opening up of freedoms within the USSR during the 1980s. True, that in 1945, 1965 and 1977 the region petitioned Moscow to unite with the Armenian SSR[23] and there were rumblings of discontent at Azeri immigration into the region, (in 1926 there were 117,000

23 The Caucasus, p.105

Armenians and 13,000 Azeris respectively; by 1979 it was 123,000 Armenians and 37,000 Azeris),[24] and the fact that Nagorno-Karabagh fell behind the Armenian SSR economically, (although not the rest of the Azerbaijani SSR), but all was muted until February 1988 when the region exploded after yet another petition accompanied by a series of rallies and strikes. This was the first serious expression of discontent within the USSR since the death of Stalin and the developments led to Azerbaijani counter demonstrations and then the gathering of more than a million people, (more than a quarter of the entire population of the Armenian SSR), in Yerevan. Feelings were running high and the authorities were paralysed in their response. This in its turn caused pogroms of Armenians in Sumgait in Azerbaijan, (thirty-two deaths – twenty-six Armenians and six Azeris).[25] The tensions continued with Gorbachev being harangued when he visited Armenia after the 1988 earthquake and pogroms in Baku in which more than ninety Armenians lost their lives.[26] An insurgency started which, in times gone by, the Red Army would have squashed without blinking but by this time the USSR itself was beginning its meltdown and by the time that it was formally dissolved on 31st December 1991, there was all-out war in Nagorno-Karabagh.

How that war was fought was dictated by two factors: geography and demography. For the Azerbaijanis it was simple: maintain a blockade around Nagorno-Karabagh to weaken the entity and stop weapons from seeping in and then advance up the broad, low-lying valley to Khankendi, (the Azeri name for Stepanakert, the region's capital). For the Armenians, they had to use their overwhelming demographic majority to force the Azeri population to flee the region and then to try and force a road link to Armenia through the former Red Kurdistan and its capital Lachin.[27] And at the same time as all of this was going on, both sides were busy courting Russian support which, in the end, proved to be crucial.

Initially Azerbaijan bombarded Stepanakert whilst the Armenians did the same, (but less successfully), with Shusha, (the only Azeri-majority city in the region). The Armenians also made a priority of capturing the Azeri village of Khojali to the east of Stepanakert as that contained Nagorno-Karabagh's only airfield. Three thousand

24 The Caucasus, p.105
25 The Caucasus, p.111
26 The Caucasus, p.113
27 The Caucasus, p.117

people lived in Khojali and in the attack 485 were killed or massacred.[28] Stunned by this, the Azerbaijan's morale fell and when the Armenians turned their attentions to a ground assault on Shusha – which the Azeris should have easily been able to defend – petrified at what their fate might be, the Azeri population merely upped and left so that on 8th to 9th May 1992, the Armenians captured the city with minimal effort. Now the entire territory of Nagorno-Karabagh was effectively Armenian but it was still blockaded on all sides and separate from Armenia proper, whilst also wide open to a full-on Azerbaijani assault. But then, only a fortnight after the catastrophe of Shusha, on 18th May 1992 the Azerbaijanis suffered another, even more calamitous, defeat with Lachin falling to the Armenians and the blockade being lifted. Now Nagorno-Karabagh had both land and air links with Armenia through which food, medicine and arms could be channelled.[29]

But then, in the summer of 1992, the tide began to change. The Azerbaijanis elected a new president, Abulfaz Elchibey and, riding a wave of patriot support and an influx of old Soviet weapons, his tanks rolled through the Armenian-populated Shaumian Region to the north of Nagorno-Karabagh and then into the region itself, capturing around 40% of the region's territory and coming within half an hour of Stepanakert itself.[30] But then the Armenians rallied and in 1993 these gains melted away as the Azerbaijani commanders began to plot against one another and the Armenians received more military support from Russia. Two of the senior Azerbaijani leaders, defence minister Rasim Gaziev and commander Suret Husseinov, plotted against the government and simply withdrew their men from the field leaving the region of Kelbajar, (part of the old Red Kurdistan buffer zone between Armenia and Nagorno-Karabagh), undefended. In April 1993 the Armenians attacked and the local population fled. The occupation of this region, never Armenian or part of Nagorno-Karabagh, drew stern international condemnation including from Turkey who closed her border with Armenia in protest. However, the largest fall-out was in Azerbaijan itself where Elchibey lost his presidency in a coup, the Soviet era leader Heidar Aliev moving to replace him. And whilst all this was happening, the Armenians simply continued to advance, causing 350,000 Azeri civilians to flee in their path.

28 The Caucasus, p.119
29 The Caucasus, p.120
30 The Caucasus, p.121

Once Aliev was established, there then began what the Armenian president Levon Ter-Petrosian referred to as "a real war" in which "both sides had real armies". Between December and February casualty figures skyrocketed, the Azerbaijanis losing around four thousand men and the Armenians two thousand. However, despite some marginal gains, Aliev's military strategy failed and both sides were exhausted. Talks began and a ceasefire came into place on 12th May 1994.[31] Minor infractions aside, it has held ever since. Thus the war ended and, holding most of Nagorno-Karabagh and seven districts of Azerbaijan proper, one has to say that the Armenians were the winners. That said, the conflict did seriously damage their international reputation and Nagorno-Karabagh then – and still today – remains unrecognised as an entity and is still officially regarded as a part of Azerbaijan.

And that was the place that we were travelling to that sunny morning. We rumbled along, firstly to Goris, a spectacularly situated town that had once been the capital of the ill-fated Republic of Mountainous Armenia and then, on its outskirts, we changed marshrutka for the journey onwards into Nagorno-Karabagh itself.

The trip contained some incredible scenery, quite different to that around Sisian and instead more like the Balkan Mountains in

31 The Caucasus, p.123-4

Bosnia or parts of Albania. The road was different too, far better maintained and engineered than all the others and large signs along it declared that it had been paid for by the Hayarstan All-Armenians Fund, a diaspora organisation that ploughs money into various Armenian projects from new classrooms for a village school to tree planting schemes to replace those felled during the electricity shortages of 1992-5. This road however, was the daddy of them all for this was the all-important artery through Lachin which allowed the Armenians to channel weapons, food and medical supplies into their beleaguered brothers and sisters in Nagorno-Karabagh. You could almost say it was the road what won it.

Near to the border we passed by the village of Tegh where, in a cliff face below the settlement, were hundreds of caves. They looked fascinating and I would have loved to have stopped but it was, of course, not possible. Later research on the internet however, revealed that many had been used for human habitation although these days only livestock dwell in them.

The border, at kink in the road in the bottom of a valley, was not what I had anticipated. For starters, there was no Armenian checkpoint whatsoever. Ok, so officially Nagorno-Karabagh isn't a proper country, I get that, but nonetheless, you are still leaving Armenian territory so why not check passports. All fuel to the fire I suppose, that Nagorno-Karabagh, which Armenia doesn't even recognise, is actually run from Yerevan.

The Nagorno-Karabagh checkpoint was, like their embassy, casual. They seemed surprised that we had bothered to buy visas – I later learnt that most people purchase them once they arrive in Stepanakert – and didn't bother to stamp our passports. I felt like saying, "C'mon guys, if you want to convince people that you're a proper country, then you should at least start acting like one!" but I didn't of course. After all, it would have been rude.

It was only a couple of miles further on, up a hefty climb, that we reached the town of Berdzor, formerly Lachin, once the grand capital of Red Kurdistan and more recently the site of some of the fiercest fighting in the war. The legacy of that was all around us in the form of bombed or burnt out buildings by the road in. nonetheless, when we got to the centre of that infamous place, it was all a bit disappointing. The capital of Red Kurdistan and flashpoint of the war was little more than a sleepy village where our driver stopped for some time to chat with "friends" in the main square after which sums of money changed hands.

After Berdzor it was a mountainous, picturesque wilderness all the way to Shushi – formerly Shusha – the Azeri stronghold during the war and formerly Nagorno-Karabagh's largest city, (Stepanakert was only made capital in 1923 at which time it was a small village). Shushi was formerly one of the great cities of the Caucasus, but today much of it lies ruined, and not for the first time either. Founded in 1747, it was called the "Jerusalem of Karabagh" due to its ethnic mix which invigorated the city making it a renowned cultural centre but which also proved to be its downfall with inter-ethnic fighting breaking out in 1905 and then again in 1920 when the Azerbaijani army sacked its Armenian Quarter leaving around five hundred dead. Ten years later, the famous Russian Jewish poet Osip Mandelstam visited and found it to be a ghost town with "forty-thousand dead windows". Afterwards Stepanakert became the region's capital and Shushi became the centre of Nagorno-Karabagh's Azeri community, hence the Armenians making its capture a priority.[32] Passing through we saw little beyond the newly-restored 19th century Armenian cathedral and two ruined mosques with fine brick minarets. Also intriguing was a working party of teenagers and twenty-somethings busy cleaning up the town's war memorial. I have read much of such "voluntary" initiatives during Soviet days and wondered if this was a continuation of the same tradition.

Stepanakert was not far from Shushi and we were dropped off in the centre where a gentleman named Ashot Simionian met us offering an apartment at 5,000 dram per person per night. We had a look and were impressed – two bedrooms, a living room, toilet and (non-working) shower, plus a large balcony which commanded a fine view over the city – and so took it. Ashot, a real businessman in the Del Boy mould, then took us to his house round the corner. Although in the heart of the city and behind a huge apartment block, it felt more like a village, being rather home-built and with a vegetable garden and a chicken run at the back. Our host bade us sit on a bench in his yard and then served us tea with berries whilst telling us about when he'd served with the Red Army in his youth, doing three years in East Germany (which he'd

32 The Caucasus, p.103-4

loved) and three in Afghanistan (understandably less keen). Both him and his house reminded me of Kolya Babamanov, the Uzbeki gent who had hosted the Lowlander and I in his house in a village not far from Urgench during our Trans-Asian trip.[33] He had also served in the Red Army, had been posted in Magdeburg in East Germany and had loved it. For all its faults, one positive of the old USSR had been its very cosmopolitan nature and the opportunities that it gave people from far-flung backwaters like Uzbekistan and Nagorno-Karabagh to enjoy experiences that they would never have had otherwise. How different I mused, are things for Ashot's children and grandchildren. He was a citizen of a superpower, the largest state on earth, which gave him the chance to cross continents; they belong to a tiny stateet, unrecognised even by its neighbours, and are barred from entering Azerbaijan, only ten miles or so down the road.

Is that what we call “progress”?

One of those disadvantaged youngsters, Ashot's son, now appeared and his father brokered a deal which would see him drive us to Gandazar Monastery, the architectural highlight of Nagorno-Karabagh, for the sum of 150 dram per kilometre, (about 20p). And so off we set in his gas-powered Volga to explore a little of this unknown and half-forgotten state.

Just outside Stepanakert we halted at Nagorno-Karabagh's most famous sight which we checked out whilst our driver went to fill up with gas. 'We Are Our Mountains' is a statue of an elderly couple, both vaguely mountain-shaped, which was erected during Soviet times to symbolise the unity of the Nagorno-Karabaghi people with their mountains. It has become the symbol of the statelet and is much-loved by all although no one refers to it by its official title; instead everyone calls it 'Mamik yel Babik' (“Granny and Granddad”).

We both liked it, a friendly, fun statue that truly succeeded where public art so often fails, in winning the hearts of minds of the people who live with it. There was a group of schoolchildren there being organised by their teacher in order to have some group photos taken in from of Granny and Granddad. All wore Young Pioneer neckties and all looked very Armenian. Well, all bar one.

33 See my travelogue 'Across Asia With A Lowlander'.

Stuck amongst his dusky-skinned and raven-haired classmates was a pale-skinned ginger lad. "Who put an Irish kid there?" asked more, for he certainly would have looked far more at home in Sligo than Stepanakert although I do know that there are a few ginger Armenians as back in Bulgaria I once taught one.

Mamik yel Babik

We wandered around the statue, had our photos taken in front of it and then descended the hill to wait for the Volga to return. On a bench beside us were a young couple, the girl in tears, and I wondered what had caused her day to be so bad.

The drive to Gandazar passed through some incredibly beautiful mountain scenery, again very Balkan and green and a world away from the bleak brown moorlands we had left that morning around Sisian. There were few signs of the conflict of two decades ago yet here there had been much fighting as this was the area that Elchibey's forces had occupied during his counterattacks following the loss of Lachin that had resulted in around 40% of the territory of Nag being taken by the Azerbaijanis. The entire population had fled in the face of the invading troops and from what I could see, there hadn't been a lot of returning since for the area was notable for its emptiness. But then Nagorno-Karabagh as a whole only has a population of 146,573 over 50,000 of which live in Stepanakert.[34] That means that less than 100,000 people are spread out across an area the size of Northern Ireland, (which has just under two million). Thus the only relics from the war that we saw were several fields with signs by them which declared that they had been cleared of mines by the HALO Trust, a non-political, non-religious NGO which is the largest humanitarian mine-clearing organisation in the world.[35]

Immediately prior to the monastery, we stopped in Gandazar village, a very spruce and prosperous looking place where everything had been painted in gaudy yellow and green for some reason giving it a Disneyland feel. That was further enhanced by an astonishingly awful Titanic-themed hotel which looked like a giant concrete liner stranded in the mountains; post-Soviet nouveau riche at its very worst! More pleasing on the eye were the brand new school and kindergarten and of interest were entire fences constructed out of old Azerbaijani number plates, they being defunct after independence, and the village souvenir shop which proudly boasted that it was run by a veteran of the war.

The Titanic Hotel

34 Wikipedia

35 Armenia with Nagorno-Karabagh, p.97

The new primary school

Numberplate heaven

High up on a mountain overlooking that most cheesy of villages was the monastery itself, one of the finest that we visited on the entire trip. It had some amazing intricate carvings particularly around the altar, but equally inspiring were the almost Alpine views from the terrace.

The altar at Gandazar

The view from the monastery

On the way back our driver tried to take us to a cheesy cave-sum-zoo tourist complex near to Gandazar village but we both refused point blank and so headed straight back to Stepanakert. There we attempted to visit the Karabagh War Museum but it was shut and so all that we could do was check out the collection of (rather primitive looking) guns outside. Then it was back to Ashot's house where we were plied with vodka and some slightly fizzy homemade wine that was not likely to win many awards whilst being treated to the most amazing meal of the entire trip – shashlik with some beautiful seasoned potatoes, tomato paste, pepper paste, vegetable and lavash.[36] Whilst eating we were pestered continually by Ashot's five-year old grandson who was an almighty pain, but, more positively, our driver opened up to us a little, telling us that he had no girlfriend and that when he was eight Azerbaijani helicopters had strafed the adjacent apartment block, upon which the pockmarks from that attack are still visible.

36 Lavash – Armenian flatbread, a delicious staple everywhere.

Ashot's yard with the Volga

As the sun was setting we bid our hosts adieu and headed to an internet café to talk with friends and family on Skype and witness Stoke City beating Newcastle United. Then, having been warmed up by Ashot, we stocked up on sausage and wine and retreated to our balcony with its magnificent view where we celebrated our arrival in this non-state by drinking into the small hours and inflicting a selection of English and Irish folk songs upon the good people of Stepanakert.

Day 6 – Stepanakert and Aghdam

We were woken around ten and neither of us felt too great which was hardly surprising given the excesses of the night before. Nonetheless, we had sights to see and, what is more, to photograph. Unfortunately though, my camera had run out of juice and its charger I had stupidly left with our luggage in Yerevan. And so there was only one thing for it: a short detour to obtain either a new charger or disposable camera before we set off.

Which was easier said than done and, despite scouring Stepanakert's finest electrical emporiums, we failed to locate what we needed. On the verge of giving up, Ashot's son tried out one last place, a tiny one-man electrical shop on Azatamartikneri Avenue and thankfully we were in luck: he could both charge the camera and flog me a multi-purpose charger. The only snag was that it would take around thirty minutes to juice it up, so I suggested that we use the time wisely by eating. We popped into a supermarket across the road, bought some lavash, sausage, sour cream and tomato paste and embarked upon a veritable feast sat on the pavement. Seeing us, the owner of an adjacent fruit and veg store came out with a little table, a knife and a complimentary tomato and cucumber, and for once we became the tourist attraction: two foreigners enjoying a picnic in the middle of the city! Afterwards, full and content, we returned the table and knife, bought some fruit to thank him for his kindness, picked up the juiced-up camera and charger and then finally set off for the place in Nagorno-Karabagh that I wanted to see more than anywhere else: Aghdam.

We headed out on the same road that we had travelled along the previous day, passing Granny and Granddad and then, several miles further on, Stepanakert's airport. This was the focus of one of the earliest battles in the war when the Armenians were still cut-off from the world and desperately needed the airport to bring in supplies. It resulted in the Khojali[37] Massacre on 25th-26th February 1992, the worst atrocity of the war. 485 people died, a good

37 Khojali was the name of the adjacent village. Today the Armenians refer to it as Ivanian.

proportion of them unarmed Azeri women and children and the Armenians must bear the brunt of the blame for this although there was also criticism inside Azerbaijan that their military did not evacuate civilians – and indeed even encouraged them to stay – due to fears that such an action would help the Armenians in their claims.[38] Nowadays, there is little evidence of the fighting and the airport boasts a brand-new terminal, completed in 2011. However, no planes fly from it. Turkey's threat to ban Armenian planes from its airspace if the airport ever opens for traffic may have something to do with it.[39]

Several kilometres on from the airport we stopped in Askeran where there were some impressive military relics to be seen although these dated back two centuries, not two decades. Mayraberd (literally "Head Fortress") was an impressive castle built in the 18th century to guard the valley leading up into Nagorno-Karabagh with fortifications on both sides of the river. Unfortunately, there are no explanatory boards detailing what was what back then so our imaginations had to take over, but it was fun scrambling over the ruins and munching fruit in the overgrown courtyard Famous Five style. More interesting for me though was seeing how wide the valley is and how near Stepanakert was to the original border, (which before the war lay at Askeran, a mere 20km from Stepanakert although these days the Nagorno-Karabaghi Army occupies a further 15km or so of Azerbaijani territory). It makes one wonder how Azerbaijan, a country with a greater population than Armenia proper, let alone Nagorno-Karabagh, ever managed to lose. Surely they could have just marched up the wide flat valley to Stepanakert and once the capital had fallen the struggle would have been largely over, especially considering that the second city, Shusha, was largely Azeri anyhow? Yet no, and whilst not wishing to belittle the efforts and sacrifices of the Armenians, surely Azerbaijani infighting and incompetence must be the main reasons behind their crushing military defeat.

38 The Caucasus, p.119

39 Wikipedia: Stepanakert Airport

Mayraberd

But whether losing the entire conflict can be blamed on Azerbaijani internal weaknesses or not, the startling landscape that we were to witness next can squarely be blamed on nothing else. Several miles on from Askeran is Aghdam, in 1991 when the Soviet Union collapsed, a thriving city of forty-thousand souls. Never in Nagorno-Karabagh territory, the war should never have even reached it, let alone should it have fallen. Yet in July 1993, whilst Azerbaijan's political elite bickered, the Armenians attacked. The civilians fled, the military put up no resistance and within hours the entire city was in Armenian hands.

Today no one lives there, not a single soul. No one can, for every building, every single building from thousands, stands completely destroyed, a pile of rubble only. Well, almost every building; one structure still stands: the city's mosque. After capturing it the Armenians meticulously blew up every home so as to prevent future pressure from the international community to allow citizens to return. And they spared the mosque so as not to be accused of religious intolerance, (the Azerbaijanis had a habit of blowing up Armenian churches).

Few sights have I seen have scorched themselves onto my mind's eye more than that of Aghdam, few vistas are as harrowing. For as far as the eye could see, across a wide and fertile plain, lay destruction, complete and utter destruction. A sea of rubble heaps that were once buildings whilst dotted around the outskirts of the town, the burnt-out, battle-scarred, rusting hulks of tanks. It was as if we had just awoken after the apocalypse or were real-life participants in some Playstation game. No one spoke.

Aghdam

But our destination that day was not Aghadam – not officially a tourist destination for obvious reasons – but instead Tigranakert, a mediaeval fortress sat amidst the ruins of an ancient city founded by King Tigran the Great (95-55BC), bang against the ceasefire line with Azerbaijan. Here, as at Khor Virap, one looked out from this tiny finger of Christianity poking into the heart of the Muslim world to a richer and more prosperous Islamic neighbour. However, unlike that sad view of Ararat, rather than thinking of lands lost, here the Christian Armenians were the aggressor who had unlawfully seized enemy territory.

Tigranakert, I am afraid to say, was a disappointment, the first of our trip. Ashot's son took us to see the ruins of an ancient church "destroyed by Azerbaijani bombs". He lied. The fact that it was set well below ground level revealed that it had been excavated by archaeologists, not blown up. And to be honest, the lies continued from there on, the whole complex having the feel of a propaganda exercise. The fort had been renovated too much, (which made me suspect that it had a double purpose as a front-line stronghold should the Azerbaijanis ever decide to attack again), whilst the exhibitions within its walls talked endlessly about how the presence of the ruins demonstrated that this had always been Armenian territory, the inference being that, despite international pressure to do so, it should never be relinquished. I found it all sad. Archaeology should not become political but when nationalists are involved, it often is.

The church "blown up" by the Azerbaijanis

We drove straight back to Stepanakert, stopping only to photograph the ruins of Aghdam, and were dropped off in the heart of the Nagorno-Karabaghi capital. We checked out Veratsnound (Renaissance) Square where the old Supreme Soviet building and new Parliament, (bizarrely attached to a hotel – imagine the Palace of Westminster with a Holiday Inn stuck on the side!), stand. It was spruce, clean and the city looked like a true capital, albeit a rather small one.

In front of the former Supreme Soviet

The Parliament with attached hotel

We walked up to where the new cathedral is being built – despite its population being very religious, there are no churches in Stepanakert at present – and then down past tawdry apartment buildings with washing hung between them, to a souvenir shop (shut), and thence the Parliament again. It was clear that the city was being done up from the centre outwards and clear too that we had seen what there was to see, so we retreated to the Armenia Hotel affixed to the Parliament and there in the terrace cafe, read books and sipped tea in a most genteel fashion. That's one of the great things about these little statelets you know: there we were, in the poshest hotel in the land, brushing shoulders with the foremost figures of the country and yet our four leisurely drinks cost only 1,000 dram (under £2).

We walked back to our apartment through a rather surreal park area which I later learnt is referred to as Lovers' Alley. A new development of nouveau riche tack, it begins with a terrace following one side of the square along which were a series of photographs showing the very best that Nagorno-Karabagh has to offer. And in amongst the predictable shots of ancient monasteries, mountains, Granny and Granddad and pretty girls in traditional costume, were a few rather bizarre ones. Some featured a number of college-age kids all dressed in Nagorno-Karabagh flag costumes dancing on stage – what was it, Nagorno-Karabagh the Musical? - but the weirdest were of two mass weddings, one at Shushi Cathedral and the other at Gandazar Monastery where we had been the day before. Hundreds of brides in white and grooms in dark suits, what was all that about? Had the Moonies suddenly become big here?

Nagorno-Karabagh the Musical?

Mass weddings at Gandazar (left) and Shushi (right)

But below the gallery of peculiar propaganda pictures led the cheesiest processional way I've ever seen, Lovers' Alley itself. There were pseudo-Classical columns and the path itself was flanked by statues of people posing except that instead of heads, they had lampshades. "Like some kind of bad Andy Warhol," commented Paul. Indeed.

Lovers' Alley

At the bottom was the smart new national stadium where Nagorno-Karabagh's national team (unrecognised by FIFA) recently beat

Abkhazia 2-0 in the great clash of nations that aren't, whilst to our right stood a Graeco-Roman pile of horrendous taste looking like a gangster's wet dream but which turned out to be Stepanakert's premier hotel, the Vallex Garden.

Strolling back to our apartment we met Ashot who arranged a car for us back to Yerevan the next day for 5,000 dram each, cheaper, quicker and more comfortable than another bloody marshrutka. He even showed us the car, a Lada no less, and we were happy. And so we relaxed, our cares removed, playing backgammon and then returning to the internet cafe of the night before to witness Liverpool beat Manchester City 3-2 to move to the top of the league. I also used the opportunity to do a bit of research and solved two mysteries.

Firstly, there was that of the mass weddings. They weren't connected to the Moonies but instead had been arranged and sponsored by Levon Hayrapetian, a local entrepreneur. On the 16th October 2008 678 couples tied the knot at Gandazar and Shushi simultaneously before attending a grand reception at the national stadium with fireworks and pop stars in attendance. Each couple was paid $2,500 each in addition to the wedding expenses. It was part of a nationwide drive to boost the population, presumably to replace those who had been killed in the conflict as well as the Azeris who had run away. In addition to private initiatives like Hayrapetian's, the government pays couples 100,000 dram for their first and second children, 500,00 for their third and 300,000 to get married, (for Armenian society is still rather conservative and the idea of supporting unmarried couples is too much for most to stomach). I just wonder where they find all the money from. Wherever it is, the mass weddings and other initiatives seem to have worked, with there being a baby boom following the weddings, the birth-rate soaring by 16% and 1,306 new Nagorno-Karabaghis entering the world in the first half of 2009.[40] But why would, money aside, anyone actually want to get married at the same time as hundreds of others? The reasons it seems, are varied. Eric Dravyan, a 25-year-old man from Stepanakert who married Karine Hayrapetyan, 20, stated that they would be holding a separate, more personal ceremony with family and friends later, whilst Vladimir Hakobjanyan, a 24-year-old from Askeran, was happy to marry his wife Noyem, 19, in that way since her parents

[40] Mass Wedding in Karabakh Results in Baby Boom

had not agreed to the match and so they couldn't have afforded to wed otherwise.[41]

And the second mystery that I solved involved a little round symbol with a swirl inside that we had seen absolutely everywhere in Armenia. On khachkars, at the start of every chapter of 'The Crossing Place' and by the door of our apartment, there was no escaping them, but what were they exactly and what do they symbolise? My research revealed those omnipresent swirly circles to be the Arevakhach, a name which literally means “solar cross”, an ancient motif Pagan and Christian, (and I suspect also Zoroastrian), which symbolises eternity and light.

And so both wiser and, I suppose, a little older, we turned in for the night.

An Arevakhach

[41] Nagorno-Karabakh: Mass Wedding Hopes to Spark Baby Boom in Separatist Territory

Day 7 – Stepanakert to Yerevan

The Lada that was to take us back to Yerevan had morphed by the morning into a marshrutka with several other passengers in it. There was no explanation for the change from Ashot but as it was half-empty, the driver was cheerful and there were no vomiting alcoholics on board, the journey was far pleasanter than the one going down. Over the next seven hours or so I gazed out of the window, finished 'The Crossing Place', devoured another laborious chunk of 'A Shameful Act' and dozed. I also clocked the important sights – the caves of Tegh, Karahunj and the mine built for the water pipes to Lake Sevan and somewhere near to Yeghegnadzor we halted for a very tasty shwarma. Descending down to the Ararat plain, Mt. Ararat itself was still shrouded in clouds but its little brother, Mini Ararat[42] was clear and visible for the first time and very pretty it was too.

Back in Yerevan we renewed our acquaintances with the manager of the dungeon hotel, retrieved our bags from the hotel laundry and then settled back into our dingy but cheap lodgings. Then, after a shower and freshen up, we were out again, taking a bus into the centre with a specific mission in mind.

We were dropped halfway along Mesrop Mashtots Avenue and from there it was a short walk along Buzand Street to the towering hulk of the 1960s post office. En route we passed through an underpass which had the following graffiti daubed on the wall in English:

42 Mini maybe, but still a whopping 3,925m tall.

MOYES IS THAT YOU? 4-1 0-3

I laughed. One has had to wait a long time for Manchester United's fall from grace, but now that it has come, it has been spectacular and all the sweeter for it. I personally hope that they languish in mid-table for decades, but that is probably asking too much. My only regret is that it has occurred under David Moyes, a manager whom I have always respected and admired.

The post office was located in a decidedly iffier part of town. Paving slabs were broken, graffiti abounded and there was a smell of urine as we climbed the stairs. Inside it appeared more like a mobile phone emporium than a centre for dealing with mail, but thankfully, unlike at Sisian, at least here we could buy some stamps. I just wonder how folk outside the capital manage to send any letters although judging by the almost total absence of any postboxes spotted anywhere, who knows, perhaps they don't?

Folk back home contacted, we were now free to enjoy the rest of the afternoon and so I suggested that we take a walk through the rather lengthy, (around 1km), pedestrian tunnel under the post office to a quirky little attraction that I'd read about in the guidebook and quite fancied seeing.

The Children's Railway is a half-sized real railway running from an idyllically-located park down along the Hravda River Gorge for a mile or so. Children's railways were a Soviet institution, not toys but fully functioning real trains that were operated by children on holidays and at weekends, the idea I suppose, being to teach all the young Ivans, Natashas, Tatyanas and Vladimirs to be good railway workers when they grew up. There were many of them built in major cities of the Union, but Yerevan's was particularly lovely with the station being a mini version of the city's own grand railway terminal, (which we hadn't visited at that point but would soon). Alas, children no longer operate the trains, but sadly one aspect of the old Soviet regime still persists: it only runs on Sundays and holidays and since the day we visited was a Monday, then we were out of luck. Oh well, next time...

We took a leisurely walk through the shaded park by the station where there was a petulant child demanding ice cream from his mother in American-accented English. She looked thoroughly embarrassed in front of her Armenian family and I was reminded of my time in Vietnam when Việt Kiều – Overseas Vietnamese, literally "Outside Vietnamese" - parents, usually from California, brought their kids over to see the motherland. It was always a shock for the kids, totally Americanised and often with an uncertain grasp (if any) of the tongue, being dumped in such a frenetic, chaotic, alien place. I recall vividly waiting for a friend to arrive at Ho Chi Minh City Airport and seeing one particular family arrive from the States. The mum and dad came first, smiling, glad to be back home, greeted by a dozen gabbling and enthusiastic relatives armed with motorbikes and mangoes, whilst following behind came two pre-pubescent kids clad in baseball caps and NBA shirts, the look on their faces saying, "What the hell is this place that you've dragged us to?" Put in such a context, perhaps the child's demanding becomes a bit more understandable although if he'd been my son, he'd have had a good, firm word.

We walked through the suburbs, past half-built hotels and hardware shops to the nearest Metro station. On the way we met a policeman who asked us if we liked Armenia and pointed the right direction for us, (the map was wrong). We hadn't tried out the Yerevan Metro before, but it was much like all the other later Soviet systems, (i.e. not those with amazingly ornate stations), and the train that we travelled in the same kind of corrugated tin can that I had travelled in on the Moscow, Tashkent, Kiev, Tbilisi, Prague, Budapest and Sofia systems.

We headed for the full-sized version of the railway station that we'd seen in the park, though not to enjoy the architecture – spectacular as it was – but instead to get the details of the trains back to Tbilisi as neither of us fancied another lengthy marshrutka ride. We got the times and the prices – a daily night train and affordable too, particularly when one took into account the fact that it saved on a night in the hotel – and so returned to the city centre with a plan.

And there we dined in our favourite cellar restaurant again before heading to Republic Square to watch the beautiful dancing fountains – and even more beautiful females of the city on their evening stroll – whilst drinking coffee and playing backgammon at the Marriott Hotel on the square, the finest-placed hotel in the land, and probably, (if the coffee is anything to go by), the most expensive also. Oh well, we were on holiday...

Day 8 – Lake Sevan

We arose at ten and breakfasted in the canteen café at the bus station, thinking that it would be convenient for what was to come next: catching a marshrutka for the thirty miles or so journey to Lake Sevan. However, upon finishing our victuals we found that there were no marshrutki from that bus station but instead they left from the West – or North, depending on who you asked – bus station which could be reached by catching a bus from a certain bus stop in town on Isahakian Street. There we headed only to be directed to a different stop on Terian Street only then to be directed back to the original stop. In the end we caught a taxi.

The Northern Bus Station was a good distance out of the city to the east on the Sevan road and from there it was not long before a marshrutka filled up and departed. Unfortunately, it filled up rather too much for my liking and so I saw little of the scenery going although what I did look at was very mountainous and brown. Instead though, I concentrated on reading, a lengthy, cheesy and very enjoyable historical romance named 'Shadow of the Moon' by one M. M. Kaye and for the hour or so that we were travelling I was more in 19th century British India than 21st century Armenia, falling in love with the dark-haired heroine Winter de Ballesteros almost as much as I was the raven-haired graces all about me on the marshrutka.

It was raining when we reached Sevan, the grimy little town on the shores of the famous lake, the first rain that we'd experienced since coming, so we hailed a taxi straightaway to escort us to Sevanavank, the ancient monastery on an “island” in the lake.

I write “island” rather than island because island is what everyone calls it when it is very plainly a peninsular, being very much connected to the mainland. However, the popular moniker is much deserved since, until very recently, Sevanavank was an island. Let me explain.

Lake Sevan is the smallest of the Three Great Lakes of Armenia. Like its highest mountains, the largest two of the three – Van and Urmia – are now irredeemably lost, Van in modern-day Turkey and Urmia within Iran. Indeed, I'd been to the shores of the former during my 2010 trip through the lost provinces of Armenia, an expanse of blue in a hot and arid land that melted into the horizon. That too had an Armenian city on the shore and church on an island. There though, both lay in ruins.

Despite being the smallest of the three lakes already, the Soviets earnestly desired to make it even smaller. Important figures had read the 1910 book by Armenian engineer Soukias Manasserian 'The Evaporating Billions and the Stagnation of Russian Capital' which put forward a scheme to reduce the depth of the lake from 95m to 45m, using the water for irrigation and hydro-electric power generation.[43] In addition to this, the new land created could be used for agricultural production, the idea being that the lake's "scraggy shores will be turned into sweet-smelling meadows, groves of nut-trees and oak trees... Around it beautiful roads and promenades will be laid... There could be no objection to diminishing the size of the lake for it would merely mean diminishing the annual evaporation of a vast quantity of moisture that rose uselessly into the air."[44]

Work began in 1933 but was delayed by the war and only completed in 1949. Declared a major achievement of the Soviet Union, lake levels began to drop by one metre a year. However, after the death of Stalin and the Secret Speech criticising him in 1956, doubts about the wisdom of the project began to be raised. The trees that were meant to be growing on the reclaimed land weren't doing all that well and fish yields from the lake – which is famous for its trout – were dropping alarmingly. In 1958 a Sevan Committee was formed to try and keep the water levels as high as possible and by 1962 the level stabilised at 18m below the original. Then a 49km tunnel was built to bring 200 million cubic metres of water each year from the River Arpa into the lake (see earlier chapter). This opened in 1981 but the water levels only rose by 1.5m so a second tunnel was cut to divert 165 million cubic metres of water per annum from the River Vorotan into the Arpa and thence the lake. This 22km megaproject, (remember the mine that I discussed earlier?), was finally completed in 2008 but by this time the water levels had dropped another two metres as, after the 1988 earthquake, the collapse of the USSR, the conflict in

43 Manasserian also produced the plan to drain the Aral Sea which has left fishing boats stranded in a salty desert and has become an ecological disaster of immense proportions. They probably have a dartboard with his face on it at Greenpeace headquarters.

44 Soviet propaganda quoted in Armenia with Nagorno-Karabagh, p.173.

Nagorno-Karabagh and the closure of the Metsamor Nuclear Power Station which provided Armenia with around half of its electricity, the hydro-electric plants sucking the water out of Lake Sevan had to increase their capacity in order to meet the electricity shortfall. Nowadays though, water levels are rising satisfactorily again and are expected to stabilise at 1,904m above sea level, only 11m below the original level. By 2009 a level of 1,899m had been reached, good news for everyone save those who built illegally on the newly-drained land by the lakeside.

It was still raining when we arrived on the peninsular island so we dived into a restaurant for tea and backgammon. Lake Sevan is, as I mentioned before, famous for its trout and the proprietor was eager for us to sample his, but after our hearty breakfast in the bus station, neither of us were hungry so we declained, planning to return later when we'd worked up an appetite. A rain shower, two games of backgammon and two teas a-piece later we were glad that we hadn't felt peckish for we were charged a whopping 4,000 dram for our tea, (the "complimentary" cakes were 1,000 dram each), and the Lord alone knows what the trout would have cost us. Both of us were angry but upon reflection, it was the only time we were ripped off on the entire trip so one shouldn't complain too much.

When the sky was clear we went down to the lakeside and took our photos with the fishing boats. We could have easily been at the seaside save for the fact that the water was fresh and there was a thin line of mountains on the distant horizon. It would have been extremely beautiful if it were not for the detritus of the tourist industry all around – shacks selling souvenirs and drinks, etc – so we walked away from the commercialised area around the car park and went to find somewhere a little more pristine.

By the fishing fleet of Lake Sevan

We didn't get very far. Only a quarter of a mile or so down the lane and we were waved back by an armed guard. The end of the island is a military zone – although what defensive purpose it serves I really struggle to comprehend – and they didn't even like us being near the fence which was a shame since the views across the placid waters were stunning. Nonetheless, I was glad to have gone that way since we passed the Soviet Writers' Guest House where the literary luminaries of the USSR once congregated to gain inspiration but which now sits crumbling and forlorn. It's a building that I'd seen on plenty of pictures, a slab of hideous 1960s modernism plonked in an ancient landscape, like putting Tracy Island from 'Thunderbirds' on Lindisfarne. As with the scheme to drain the lake that it overlooked, it spoke of an arrogant and insensitive time.

Insensitive: The Writers' Rest House with the monastery behind

We climbed the hill to the monastery itself though, after visiting several of Armenia's more spectacular churches, I was not expecting much, particularly as my guidebook described it disparagingly as "not really one of Armenia's most appealing places and [it] owes its popularity largely to its proximity to the lake and its accessibility from Yerevan."[45] Yet the two tiny extant churches pleasantly surprised us both. Whilst no competition architecturally for Echmiadzin, Gandazar, Syuni or even Khor Virap, they were exquisite in their intimate, earthy humbleness and the location was breath-taking.

I went into the larger of the two churches, the Mother of God Church where I met its extremely friendly caretaker. It turned out that he was a coin collector which meant that we had something in common as I collect banknotes. He asked about British coins and after much rummaging through our pockets, Paul and I managed to locate 1p, 2p, 5p, 10p, 20p and 50p pieces which we then fitted together to demonstrate how they form the image of a complete Royal Standard. This must be quite unique in world numismatics as he was most impressed and even more so when we presented

45 Armenia with Nagorno-Karabagh, p.175

them to him as a gift. In thanks, he showed us his church's greatest treasure, an incredible 13th century khachkar which depicted – amongst other things – the Four Evangelists, the Three Kings, Adam and Eve and, most fascinating of all, Christ with His hair braided in Mongol style as it was at that time that Genghis Khan's men were sweeping through Asia destroying all in their path. It was an amazing work of art and snapshot of history and having it explained to us by such an enthusiastic gentleman made it all the more powerful to us.

The Mongol Christ

I sat and prayed in the small and older Holy Apostles Church for some time. It was my favourite church in all Armenia and, perhaps significantly, also the smallest and humblest that we'd entered. Only fitting for the worship of a humble carpenter I suppose.

Afterwards I climbed the hill to its crest and sat there for some time. The 360° views over the entire lake were breath-taking and much more so because of the stark contrast with Yerevan only 30 miles or so away. There all is dusty and brown, it is warm enough to wear shorts and a T-shirt and to drink coffee outdoors after sundown. At the lake though, it was chilly even with a coat on and snow still lay on most of the slopes. The lake itself was a placid, glassy deep blue but the mountains which surround it were dark. The only place which bore any similarity to it was the landscape around Sisian and the only other area in the world that I could compare it to are the wilder, bleaker moors of Scotland, Wales and England, yet even so, there was something subtly different between here and there: it was familiar yet also very alien.

Sevanavank

Lake Sevan

Sat on that hilltop, I made a short video reflecting on the entire trip around Armenia which was now beginning to draw to a close. There was a lot to reflect on for Armenia packs so much into such a tiny country, both human and physical. I have just discussed how radically different the landscapes around Lake Sevan and Sisian are to Yerevan yet they were only two of several that we'd witnessed on our journeyings. The incredibly brown Debed Valley on the way in that was almost Albanian; th peaks and valleys of Nagorno-Karabagh that could have been in the Carpathians of the mountains of Bosnia and then that flat, fertile plain on which stood the ruins of Aghdam, almost Dutch from a distance.

But the physical geography was only half of it and, although I know this sounds like a cheesy cliché, it is her people that make Armenia so special. Their native art style is truly unique, at times Persian, at times almost Islamic, then somehow Celtic yet always wholly Armenian; the national church which is instantly recognisable and both independent and different from any other church on the planet, and then the great city of Yerevan which must rate as one of the most cultured and civilised capitals on the planet. And once you've finished looking at all that then there's the women, oh the women...

As I sat there I noticed two lovers in embrace lower down the slope, oblivious to the world as they gazed into one another's eyes, their forms silhouetted against the glittering waters of the lake. It was a beautiful and timeless image and an honour to be able to witness it. I just hope that they don't mind that I captured them for all eternity with my camera.

Love

We ummed and arred over what to do once we had descended the hill. We'd seen what we had come to see but it was still early. Around fifteen miles down the shore of the lake lay the Field of Khachkars, the finest collection of cross stones in all Armenia with just under a thousand dating from all era of Armenian history. The guidebook raved about it, calling it a highlight of the land, but we had seen a hell of a lot of khachkars already and wondered what seeing a load more would give us. In the end though, after some debate, the lack of alternatives made us decide to get a taxi out to them, agreeing a price of 6,000 dram for the trip.

The drive along the water's edge was fascinating and as we rode realised just how far reality had proved to be from the Soviet vision of "sweet-smelling meadows, groves of nut trees and oak trees" with "beautiful roads and promenades". The whole scene was instead bleak, not helped by the spitting rain and melting snow I admit, but nonetheless, the road was bumpy rather than beautiful, the land by the shore bare or dotted with straggly bushes and the buildings dilapidated. The scene reminded me more of Kazakhstan or some other Central Asia republic than a lakeside paradise.

Not quite paradise: Driving by Lake Sevan

We passed by the town of Gazar, formerly Nor Bayazit – New Bayazit – where the refugees from that now Turkish – or to be more ethnically accurate, Kurdishj – city fled to. I'd stayed in their old home four years before and seen the ruins of the Armenian town although, ironically, the whole city had now been relocated a mile or so to the west and the new settlement is now named Doğubayazıt which translates as, you've guessed it, New Bayazit.

The Field of Khachkars, an immense cemetery near to the lake's edge, reminded me of an ancient churchyard in North or Mid Wales somewhere, but that may just have been because of the drizzle. It was a remarkable place and we spent a good half an hour there wandering amongst the khachkars and photographing some of the more interesting ones, but our earlier fears were realised and there are only so many carved stones that a man can truly appreciate and we had already reached our limit.

Khachkars

On the way back our driver stopped to fill-up with gas and afterwards I took the opportunity to solve the gas rather than petrol mystery. The answer was simple: in Armenia petrol sells at 500 dram per litre whilst gas is 250 dram. Most of that gas comes from Russia, (and a little from Iran), whom Armenia is friendly with unlike its northern neighbour Georgia. But how did this gas get through considering the Turkish and Azerbaijani blockades to the west and east and Georgia being in the way to the north. "Bribes sort that out," was the explanation given. This prompted a then and now conversation and our driver, a man in his forties, was adamant that things were better when Armenia had been a part of the USSR. People had jobs and money then; now the roads are awful. Gorbachev, in his opinion, "fucked everyone up the arse".

Filling up with gas

In Sevan, perhaps the grottiest town in all Armenia, the roads were truly awful, the main streets being more like a farm track. And to make it worse, when we got there, the last marshrutka back to the capital had already left. We negotiated a price of 7,000 dram with our driver and headed back by car which was much pleasanter than the journey going as we were now able to see the scenery as we dropped around a thousand metres back down to the plain. As he drove our driver continued with the corruption theme, talking about hotels owned by the president's brother and pointing out a gangster's mansion on the edge of the city that was built to look like a church and was where Dmitri Medvedyev had stayed a year or two before.

In the capital we met up with the boys that we'd got acquainted with before our jaunt down to Nagorno-Karabagh. They arrived with friends and all were football-mad – good for me but less so for Paul who, as a Munster man, prefers the other shaped ball. There was Aram who supported Manchester United, Alfred an AC Milan aficionado and David who liked Arsenal. We walked around the streets, talked largely of the beautiful game but also of the boring architecture on the new Northern Avenue,[46] with lashings of macho gesturing and a sad, yet predictable, burst of homophobia which is de rigeur in that area of the world. We showed them the David Moyes graffiti which Alfred and David found funny, Aram less so, and then we retired to a sports bar to watch the semi-final of the German domestic cup between Borussia Dortmund and Wolfsburg. This was a popular game amongst the locals since Armenia's star striker, their best player for a generation or more, Henrikh Mkhitaryan, was playing up front for Dortmund and the bar was offering a 15% discount on all drinks if he scored. Anyway, the boys proved to be excellent company and we had a good night indeed, particularly when Mkhitaryan did score and the whole place erupted in cash-saving jubilation.

Drinks with the footie mad lads

When we got back to our hotel we found two other travellers had checked-in next door. They were the first other backpackers that we'd seen all trip and we soon fell into conversation. Filip and Vilem were a pair of Czechs with a passion for mountaineering and

---

46 The Northern Avenue was part of Tamanian's original masterplan that was never constructed. In 2002 work controversially started to complete the great man's vision and it is now open to the public, a broad new boulevard linking Republic Square with the Opera House. However, it has attracted much criticism due to the standard of its buildings being far below the quality of those built by Tamanian and the corners cut during construction.

another for alcohol. They'd just arrived from Georgia where they'd tried – and failed – to climb Mt. Kazbek and met a couple of "fun" Ukrainian girls on the bus. They were good company and so we talked and drank into the small hours although when Paul went to the toilet, Filip asked as to why he had no trouble understanding my English but struggled with that of my friend. "You know how a Slovak speaks Czech," I replied and they nodded in understanding.

And more drinks with the Czechs in our dungeon

Day 9 – Garni and Geghard

We were up at ten with a hangover on our last day in Armenia. We'd arranged with the taxi driver who'd escorted us back from the centre one night to take us to Garni Temple and Geghard Monastery, two of Armenia's most famous sights and both within easy reach of Yerevan. We'd chosen this driver as he was friendly, intelligent and spoke good English due to having lived for many years overseas in Germany, Syria, Jordan and Kazakhstan, being a fully-qualified dentist, (which made me wonder quite what he was doing driving taxis).

We headed out of Yerevan and into the hills. Vilem and Filip thought that the best way to cure a hangover was to drink more and were passing beer about. To their annoyance, I refused stubbornly, though Paul partook. The fact is, I like a drink as much as anyone but before 5pm all it ever seems to do is send me to sleep and this was not a day that I wanted to doze through.

Rounding one corner, Filip exclaimed, "What mountain is that?" and looking to where he was pointed, we all got our first view of the trip of Ararat in all her glory. Shrouded by clouds at Khor Virap and Yerevan and on the journeys to and fro Nagorno-Karabagh, Paul and I had resigned ourselves to not seeing her in full yet there, on our very last day in the country, she shimmered in all her volcanic magnificence. What a fitting finale and what a sight! We stopped immediately for photographs before continuing on our way.

Ararat

I liked the temple at Garni. The setting was spectacular, above a gorge, surrounded by almost Mediterranean hills. Pride of place though went to the temple itself, a slice of Ancient Rome plonked in the Caucasus. It was as if we had just stepped into an Asterix & Obelix adventure.

And perhaps about as historically accurate. Garni is the best preserved Roman building in the Caucasus, a complete Pagan temple dating back to the 1st century and once dedicated to Mithras. Well, maybe. Actually, most of it is a rebuild or even a reimagining. The original was largely destroyed in an earthquake back in 1679 and what you see now is the product of a reconstruction between 1969 and 1975. As to how authentic that reconstruction is, historians differ; some even believe that Garni never was a temple at all and instead the tomb of a Romanised local ruler. How tragic it is when our illusions are shattered so! Nonetheless, it was a great place to visit, not only for the temple itself, (which could, after all, be an accurate rebuild), but also for the remains of a (definitely authentic) bathhouse with a spectacular mosaic which contains the words, "We worked but did not get anything". In his classic travelogue of the USSR 'Among the Russians', Colin Thubron patronisingly notes that "a tour-leader pointed them out to his group as proof of Capitalist oppression of mosaic-workers in the first century AD and shrivelled the life-loving fantasy beneath our feet to Marxist dust."[47] Maybe, although I somehow doubt that Mr. Thubron has ever had to put up with the oppression that such Marxists strive to halt. Indeed, if his publishers had refused to pay him a penny after selling thousands of his books, would his words have been any different to those of the oppressed 1st century mosaic artists? I somehow suspect not.

Garni

Our next stop, the famous cave monastery at Geghard, was only a few miles further on from Garni. I'd wanted to visit this place ever since watching Ian Wright stroll around it on the Lonely Planet episode on Armenia and Georgia.[48]

And it did not disappoint. Set in the end of a narrow river valley, the hills rocky and bare, the monastery initially looked little different to most of the others. However, inside it bore no similarities to all

47 Among the Russians, p.177

48 Lonely Planet Series 7, Episode 2: Georgia & Armenia (2001)

we had seen before as most of the church was actually built into the hill, utilising ancient caves which had been further hollowed out and decorated with carved stonework. It was an incredibly atmospheric place and I enjoyed sitting in peace for a while with a candle. Afterwards I explored the monks' cells, tiny cave chambers where devout men would live for years, and then an upper chamber of the church which had the most amazing acoustics that I have ever experienced. I stood in the centre of the room and sang a verse of 'Veni, Veni, Emmanuel' and it was as if an entire choir were accompanying me.

Inside the cave church

On the way back to our taxi I decided to try out some of the snacks being offered by the hawkers outside the monastery compound. We'd seen the same stuff on sale everywhere that we went but had been apprehensive about trying them as they all looked, well... suspect. The main one was a sort of brown, gooey string with blobs on it. This turned out to be a string of nuts covered in, well, gooey brown stuff, but it was rather tasty. The other Armenian snack staple was a sort of piece of brown paper that turned out to be dried apricot puree rolled into sheets. They call it “fruit” or “sour lavash” and of the two it was my favourite.

We made only one stop on the way back to the hotel and that was due to Paul who was still suffering from the excesses of the night before – and, no doubt, Vilem's early morning beers – and had to empty the contents of his stomach by the side of the road. Taking his condition into account, we rested awhile upon our return before heading into Yerevan, bidding our Czech friends adieu at the foot of the Cascade and then taking the Metro to the grand railway terminal to buy our tickets onwards to Tbilisi that evening. We decided to treat ourselves and go first class and, at a mere 17,000 dram each, why not? Although still a grand place, Yerevan's railway station felt a bit sad and empty. Once connected to the greatest railway system on earth, with lines running from Vladivostok to Brest, Archangel to Dushnabe and thence connections onwards to destinations all over Europe and Asia. Nowadays though, it only serves a few trains per day. The main trunk line to Iran is now severed at the sleepy town of Yeraskh due to Azerbaijani Nakhijevan blocking the way south whilst closed borders to the east and west mean no expansion is possible in those directions. So, the only line of any real importance is the one that we would be travelling along, to Tbilisi though via a very roundabout route through Armavir and Gyumri which means that a marshrutka or bus is several hours quicker, and even this line can only get you into Georgia as the routes onwards to the north are severed due to the frosty relations between Russia and Georgia and the breakaway Republic of Abkhazia through which the only mainline to Moscow passes. So, aside from a few local services, there is but the night train to Tbilisi which leaves every other day, returning the following night.

Tickets bought, we headed into beautiful Yerevan one last time to while away the hours playing backgammon, writing postcards, checking the internet and admiring the ladies. Then it was time to go so we headed back to that station of stations, (still largely empty) where I finally finished 'A Shameful Act' and then got told off by a soldier for whistling a tune, ("Give a man a hat..." Paul commented), before finally boarding the train. I've been on several of the great old Soviet trains before, but for Paul it was a new experience. Thankfully, some things have improved over the years and, unlike when the Lowlander and I travelled through Uzbekistan, there was no attempt to fill-up our compartment with either non-registered passengers or contraband melons.[49] And so,

49 See my travelogue 'Across Asia With A Lowlander'.

as the sun sank behind the slopes of Ararat, we rumbled out of the station and the magical and ancient land of Armenia.

The Tbilisi Train

Postscript – A Georgian Minibreak

The train rolled into Tbilisi Railway Station at a ten to eight in the morning. Bleary-eyed, we alighted, checked our bags into left luggage and then changed some of our pounds into Georgian lari before heading north on the Metro to the Didube Bus Station. I knew Tbilisi a little after having spent several days there in 2010,[50] and that was why I headed for Didube as Didube Bus Station is where the marshrutki for all over Georgia leave from.

The word "marshrutka" (plural "marshrutki") comes from the Russian "marshrutnoe taksi" (routed taxi) which itself comes from the German "Marschroute", a combination of "walk" or "march" and "route". I hadn't liked them the first time that I'd learnt the term back in Didube Bus Station four years before and nothing in the meantime had conspired to improve my image of them, but we needed to head places and last time around I'd learnt that, in Georgia, the train is a far worse option.

We were splitting up, Paul and I. Partially because I had already seen the city that he wished to explore and partly because I enjoy my own company and, whilst Paul had been an excellent travelling companion over the last couple of weeks, I desperately wanted some time alone. Which was all well and good except that, unlike me, Paul hadn't been to Georgia before, couldn't read Cyrillic and didn't speak any Russian. So it was that I found him the marshrutka for Gori, gave him the guidebook so he'd know how to get about once there and then sought my own transport further west to Borjomi.

Gori is Stalin's birthplace and, after the great man's death, Beria turned the city into a virtual shrine to him. I'd visited in 2010, made friends with the stationmaster and thoroughly enjoyed my sojourn there. Around 80km west from his hometown, in a gorge cut by the Mtkvari River, lies another town associated with old Uncle Joe. Borjomi was the old dictator's favourite spa and since I sought

50 See my travelogue 'Latvia, Georgia and Turkey 2010'.

some and love spas then, well, was I going to head anywhere else?

I left Tbilisi with me feeling that we were in a very different country to the one that I had left the night before. The Georgians looked different to their southern brethren – still dark features but lighter skin, more European features and, I am afraid to say, much plainer females. Their faith is different too; icons abounded everywhere and whenever a church was passed everyone devotedly crossed themselves thrice, back-to-front. Georgia is the most openly and passionately Orthodox country that I have ever visited. It is also poorer and scruffier than Armenia, (Sevan excepted), but the roads were much better. It reminded me of Romania and Bulgaria in the 1990s. Overall Romania had far greater poverty than Bulgaria, but in amongst the chaos and rubbish there were unexpected signs of wealth that could only be dwelt of south of the Danube, like brand-new high speed trains and the impressive Bucharest Metro.

The marshrutka left Tbilisi behind and passed Mtskheta, the Echmiadzin of Georgia, with its grand stone cathedral, and then veered westwards along a new, smooth and largely-empty dual-carriageway.

The road did not run along the floor of the Mtkvari Valley as the railway does, but instead a mile or so to the north. As we passed Gori it commanded fantastic views over the city and I could pick out the citadel and Stalin Museum that I had visited on my last trip. I just hoped that Paul would enjoy them as much as I had done. Also of interest was a close-up view of the IDP[51] settlement that I had spied from the citadel before and an enormous military base to the north of the city close by the highway. Both were there because, less than a mile north of the road, lies South Ossetia, the region that declared its independence from Georgia during the 2008 conflict when the Russians invaded and occupied Gori itself for a few days. If things kick-off again in Georgia, this is the spot where it is most likely to happen.

After Khashuri, a nondescript town some fifty kilometres on from Gori, the valley narrowed and became very picturesque, the scenery changing from wide Central Asian brown expanse to

51 Internally Displaced Persons

almost Alpine slopes and greens. Soon we were in Borjomi itself, the main settlement in those parts, and at the bus station I summoned a taxi and asked the driver to find me some suitable accommodation. He took me over the Mtkvari and up a steep hill to a private house where rooms were being rented out at 30 lari per night. The one that I was shown was good and the location pleasant and so I took it and slumped thankfully on the bed, tired of all the travel.

I took a walk around the town which really was a charming place indeed. I'd wanted to visit back in 2010 but hadn't had time and so I was glad to have the chance to do so now. I crossed back over the river and then followed two ladies dressed in long black skirts and headscarves, the attire of religious Orthodox women, to the former Hotel Borjomi, a huge ex-Inturist concrete slab at the eastern end of the town now full of refugees from Abkhazia, the other Georgian province which has broken away from its parent country and declared independence, (like South Ossetia, with considerable Russian assistance). It was a sorry-looking place, with washing hanging from the balconies, a slice of misery in the midst of an Alpine paradise. Having just come from Nagorno-Karabagh this place provided the flip-side view of such post-Soviet unrecognised entities. Like with Nagorno-Karabagh, (and South Ossetia and Transdniestra), the majority of the population of Abkhazia had wished for independence, usually because of a culture of aggressive nationalism in the parent country, but there were also those who wished to maintain the status quo and were thus forced out of the land where their families had dwelt for generations. Doubtless, there are similar sorry hovels full of refugees across Azerbaijan peopled by the former inhabitants of those now sorry and broken ruins that we had seen at Aghdam. I wondered what stories those two traditionally-attired girls could tell, which village they had been forced from, what cottage, vegetable garden and orchard they had left behind.

The Mtkvari with the former Hotel Borjomi in the background

Having seen the dark side of Borjomi, I headed to the town's museum to explore its history. On the way I saw more evidence of the local religiosity: an elderly priest was walking the streets and passers-by were coming up to him and asking for blessings. Although undoubtedly religious, we had witnessed nothing like that in Armenia and whilst from a distance the Armenian and Georgian churches may appear to the stranger to be much the same, in actual fact they are markedly different in many areas aside from how they view the Council of Chalcedon.

Borjomi's museum was a delight. Housed in a rambling – and crumbling – villa once owned by the Romanovs, it contained a variety of artwork, stuffed animals and artefacts. I found of particular interest the sections of the town's bid to host the 2014 Winter Olympics and a gallery sponsored by BP on local archaeological finds, (whilst building a pipeline through the area, the oil giant had paid for archaeological digs and restored an ancient church which I would have loved to have had the chance to visit).

After the museum I walked to the spa itself. On the way I passed the railway station which now hosts a restaurant, the Metropol, where I decided to dine. The bowl of kharcho, (a traditional Georgian dish that contains mutton, garlic, rice and vegetables in a spicy soup), was excellent – Armenian food is good, but Georgian is world-class – but the waitress, a young lady named Maiya, was the most miserable that I have ever come across.

The spa is located in a park about a kilometre from the town centre. It was a lovely walk, past a string of traditional Georgian villas with incredible fretwork. One had been restored and is now the headquarters of the Borjomi Spa Water Company whose products are seen on tables all across Georgia and beyond, (it was once the most popular mineral water in the USSR),. By the park gates a new hotel was being built but it was not distasteful and when it is finished and the whole promenade by the river completed, the area will be very pleasant indeed.

The Spa at Borjomi

I paid a nominal fee to enter the park which was well-maintained initially but got tattier the further I ventured in. After half a mile or so it petered out entirely but I continued walking through the beautiful forested gorge to the public bath set in a meadow in the middle of the mountains, away from any civilisation.

It was an incredible place, one of the most beautiful bathing spots that I have ever visited, marred only by the litter left by previous visitors. There were few other people there then, al locals, including one charming wide-hipped girl, but after twenty minutes or so they all left and I had the place entirely to myself save for the presence of a few grazing cows. I submerged myself in the glorious sulphurous water lazily, feeling that life couldn't get any better. There is no pleasure on earth greater than that of bathing in a spa and few spas as marvellous as that one with regards to setting.

The bathing pool in the woods

I strolled back through the woods to the park where I imbibed two pints of water from Stalin's favourite spring. It was slightly warm, very sulphurous and tingly and although I enjoyed it, I couldn't have drank anymore. Then I made my way back to the Metropol where I dined again, this time on chakapuli, a stew of lamb, scallions and greens with tarragon. It was again excellent and Maiya again morose and what is more, the CD again the same, three songs on loop, one of which was James Blunt's 'You're Beautiful' which is a nice song once or twice but rather grating after ten plays.

Back up the steep hill to my room, I fell into conversation with the owner, a friendly chap who had lived for ten years in the USA and boasted of visiting no less than twenty-five states. He admitted to missing his life there somewhat, but then moved onto talking about currency exchange rates, being much impressed by the strength of pound sterling. As we talked a car pulled up and out got the pretty wide-hipped girl from the bathing pool who said hello and turned out to be his daughter.

That evening, after the sun had set, I walked down into the town to buy some water. Borjomi truly is a beautiful place by night as much as by day. I passed a fantastic pseudo-Gothic castle which turned out to be a former palace of the Romanovs, Borjomi being a magnet for all the great and good in the old imperial days, attracting such luminaries as Chekov and Tchiakovsky as well as Stalin and a number of tsars. On mountain slopes above the town, several large crosses were illuminated in neon providing spiritual guidance in the blackness. It was a friendly place too. After I'd bought the water and a few snacks from the supermarket, I saw my taxi driver who waved hello. Only in town a few hours and already feeling part of the family! It was nice, a fantastic and relaxing end to the trip and I was a happy man as I ascended back up the hill to my room where I finished 'Shadow of the Moon' before turning in for the night.

I was up early the following morning to catch the nine o'clock marshrutka back to Tbilisi. I would have dearly loved to have spent several days relaxing and walking in the hills about Borjomi but it was not possible and at least I had been lucky enough to experience it once. Maybe next time...?

On the way back to the capital I read from cover to cover a rather strange Japanese novel named 'Hotel Iris' by one Yoko Ogawa which I found rather enjoyable although in my mind's eye reality mixed with fiction and whilst the overall setting was definitely a rather sleepy Japanese seaside resort, the hotel itself was the eccentric edifice of Borjomi Museum.

Upon arrival I took the Metro to the railway station where I dropped my overnight bag and then made my way to Freedom Square, the heart of the city. I'd decided to check out the National Museum not having managed to do so on my last visit, but it was shut, the day being Good Friday. Not realising that it was such a holy day, (to be fair, I think the Georgian Church uses a different calendar to the Anglican), I popped into the adjacent Kashveti Church. To be fair, as churches go, this one was nothing remarkable, only dating from the early 20th century, but I must admit that I enjoyed being in a church with plenty of icons.

I wandered along Rustaveli Avenue back to Freedom Square and then down Pushkin Street towards the river. That whole area had been extensively renovated since my last visit, the traditional wooden houses with fretwork balconies that have a flavour of New Orleans looking spruce and handsome, whilst below them the old city walls had been excavated and imaginatively presented.

I stopped to buy presents in a market and then dined on kharcho and garlic aubergine in a little restaurant before continuing on to the river itself, my intention to head to the old city. I never got that far however, as I spied a fascinating-looking church which turned out to be the Anchiskhati Church, the oldest in all Tbilisi. I went inside and found a real gem. Dating from the 6th century with chunky Romanesque pillars, it had a smattering of worshippers inside as the priests busied themselves preparing for the service of Divine Liturgy. I went around kissing the icons and then waited as the Liturgy commenced. It was indescribably beautiful, an earthy, sweet Orthodoxy that soothes the senses and brings one closer to God. I stayed for some time stood by a pillar, (there are few chairs in Orthodox churches), soaking up the Divine Liturgy until it grew so crowded that one could hardly move.

Inside the Anchiskhati Church

Then I went on my way, retreating to a cafe adjacent to a strange, crooked, ancient-looking clocktower, (but which I suspect must be brand-new as it is not mentioned in my (2007) guidebook. There I sipped tea and began writing a short story inspired by a trip earlier in the year along the Heart of Wales Line[52] whilst all the while I could still hear the haunting Liturgy being chanted in the background.

The curious clocktower

After my tea I walked through the Old City. There was evidence of much renovation since 2010 and Tbilisi is fast becoming a very pleasant city indeed. I went shopping for a hat; not any old hat but a very specific one. Back in 2010 I'd bought one from a roadside vendor when my marshrutka had stopped en route to Kazbegi. The hat in question was a knitted woollen one decorated with crosses all the way around. Despite having a number of slightly ridiculous hats in my possession, I had never come across one that was quite 'me'. Or at least, not until that marshrutka stopped that fateful day. The hat was comfy, stylish in an "I'm not stylish whatsoever" kind of way and, most importantly of all, something of a talking

52 Caertomos

point, (Matt, where on earth did you get *that*?!"). I wore it everywhere until, on a trip to St. David's earlier in the year, I left it behind by accident. Since then I had been hatless, almost naked wherever I roamed. How fortuitous therefore, that I had already booked another trip to Georgia to replace it.

The hat in question was a traditional Georgian design, but although there were no shortage of traditional Georgian hats on sale in all the souvenir shops, all were of a very different, far sillier and furrier type. I guessed that my hat was probably only traditional in a certain region, (that around Kazbegi I assume), whilst these dafter headpieces were from a different region. However, after extensive and dedicated searching, I did locate a shop near to Freedom Square with a much wider hat selection and I bought several ensuring that my hat may be properly clad for years to come.

Beer advert showing a trio of Georgian hats. The ones on sale everywhere were like that on the left; mine is like the one on the right

I made my way back to the railway station where I passed the time writing the short story and drinking Natakhtari Pear Lemonade, a firm favourite from my first visit. After an hour or so Paul arrived and, after catching up on each other's activities – he had *really* enjoyed Gori – we made our way back to the Old Town so that he could see a little of the highlights of the capital. We walked through the narrow streets to the river where a swish new bridge leads to a brand-new park. Once again, it was clear that there had been substantial investment in improving Tbilisi in recent years and the city that I had been lukewarm about in 2010 I was now really beginning to like.

And the greatest of all those improvements led from the newly laid-out park to the imposing statue of Mother Georgia, (a sister of Mother Armenia in Yerevan and Mother Ukraine in Kiev), stood on the Sololaki Ridge which runs to the west of the Old Town. This was a brand-new cablecar which whisked us up, over and above the city on an amazing journey, before depositing us at the feet of the great woman herself and next to the Narikala Citadel. Foyur years before I'd scrambled up the hill in the intense summer heat to the citadel only to discover nondescript ruins and a hawker selling lukewarm bottled mineral water. This was far more civilised!

Mother Georgia herself (Kartlis Deda in Georgian) is, like her Armenian sister, an impressive lady, a twenty metre high aluminium statue carrying a sword in one hand and a bowl in the other. Constructed between 1958 and 1963, her choice of objects to hold demonstrates that Georgia is hospitable but also ready to defend herself. Stood at her feet though, she was not the main attraction, but instead the city itself, laid out like a carpet below us, glittering in the spring sunlight.

Paul overlooking Tbilisi

And there we finished our Georgian minibreak and indeed, our entire Caucasian odyssey. We'd no more energy or head space left for sightseeing and only wanted to soak up the atmosphere and relax for the few remaining hours until our plane departed back to Amsterdam. After all, there'd be little chance to do either when we got back home. And it had been a good trip, for Paul all had been new, for me a mix of both the alien and the familiar, but enjoyable in equal measure. The South Caucasus are home to some of the most ancient and fascinating human civilisations on earth and it packs a lot into a very small space, (Georgia is roughly the same size as the Republic of Ireland whilst Armenia is smaller). What is more, very few people seem to have cottoned on to just how brilliant it is. Which for me, is not a problem at all.

Georgia: It's all about the Natakhtari Pear Lemonade and Borjomi Water

Written Hanley, Stoke-on-Trent, 9th December, 2014

Bibliography

Books

Among the Russians: From the Baltic to the Caucasus
Colin Thubron
Published by Heinemann Ltd. (London, UK) 1983

Armenia with Nagorno-Karabagh (Edition 3)
Nicholas Holding with Deirdre Holding
Published by Bradt Travel Guides Ltd. (Chalfont St. Peter, UK) 2011

The Crossing Place
Philip Marsden
Published by Flamingo (London, UK) 1994 (First edition: 1993)

Georgia (Edition 3)
Tim Burford
Published by Bradt Travel Guides Ltd. (Chalfont St. Peter, UK) 2007

A Shameful Act: The Armenian Genocide and the Question of Turkish Responsibility
Taner Akçam
Published by Constable Ltd. (London, UK) 2007

Articles

Mass Wedding in Karabakh Results in Baby Boom
Azbarez.com 20/08/2009
http://asbarez.com/69565/mass-wedding-in-karabakh-results-in-baby-boom/

Nagorno-Karabakh: Mass Wedding Hopes to Spark Baby Boom in Separatist Territory
Eurasianet.org 23/10/2008
http://www.eurasianet.org/departments/insightb/articles/eav102408.shtml

www.ingramcontent.com/pod-product-compliance
Ingram Content Group UK Ltd.
Pitfield, Milton Keynes, MK11 3LW, UK
UKHW020241250726
13967UKWH00001B/484

9 780244 043810